Integrating Computer Science Across the Core: Strategies for K–12 Districts

Integrating Computer Science Across the Core is a guide to systematizing computer science and computational thinking practices in your school. While most books explain how to teach computer science as a stand-alone discipline, this innovative approach will help you leverage your existing curriculum to deepen and expand students' learning experiences in all content areas. Effective, equitable, and sustainable, this blueprint provides principals, curriculum directors, directors of technology, and other members of your school or district leadership team with suggested organizational structures, tips for professional learning, and key resources like planning instruments.

Tom Liam Lynch is Director of Education Policy at the Center for New York City Affairs and Editor-in-Chief of InsideSchools.org at The New School, USA, and a former education technology professor, English teacher, and school district official for the New York City Department of Education.

Gerald Ardito is Associate Professor of Computer Science Education at Manhattanville College, USA. He was previously a middle school science teacher and Assistant Professor of STEM-D Education at Pace University, USA.

Pam Amendola is an English teacher at Dawson County High School in Dawsonville, Georgia, and previously taught British and American literature at Brookwood High School in Snellville, Georgia, USA.

Other Eye On Education Books Available from Routledge
(www.routledge.com/eyeoneducation)

Making Technology Work in Schools:
How PK-12 Educators Can Foster Digital-Age Learning, 2nd Edition
Tim D. Green, Loretta C. Donovan, and Jody Peerless Green

Reinventing Crediting for Competency-Based Education:
The Mastery Transcript Consortium Model and Beyond
Jonathan E. Martin

Tech Request:
A Guide for Coaching Educators in the Digital World
Emily L. Davis and Brad Currie

Coding as a Playground:
Programming and Computational Thinking in the Early Childhood Classroom
Marina Umaschi Bers

Universal Design for Learning in the Early Childhood Classroom:
Teaching Children of all Languages, Cultures, and Abilities, Birth – 8 Years
Pamela Brillante and Karen Nemeth

Intentional Innovation:
How to Guide Risk-Taking, Build Creative Capacity, and Lead Change
J. Juliani

7 Steps to Sharing Your School's Story on Social Media
Jason Kotch and Edward Cosentino

Integrating Computer Science Across the Core

Strategies for K–12 Districts

Tom Liam Lynch, Gerald Ardito, and Pam Amendola

NEW YORK AND LONDON

First published 2020
by Routledge
52 Vanderbilt Avenue, New York, NY 10017

and by Routledge
2 Park Square, Milton Park, Abingdon, Oxon, OX14 4RN

Routledge is an imprint of the Taylor & Francis Group, an informa business

© 2020 Taylor & Francis

The right of Tom Liam Lynch, Gerald Ardito, and Pam Amendola to be identified as authors of this work has been asserted by them in accordance with sections 77 and 78 of the Copyright, Designs and Patents Act 1988.

All rights reserved. No part of this book may be reprinted or reproduced or utilised in any form or by any electronic, mechanical, or other means, now known or hereafter invented, including photocopying and recording, or in any information storage or retrieval system, without permission in writing from the publishers.

Trademark notice: Product or corporate names may be trademarks or registered trademarks, and are used only for identification and explanation without intent to infringe.

Library of Congress Cataloging-in-Publication Data
A catalog record for this title has been requested

ISBN: 978-0-367-19862-6 (hbk)
ISBN: 978-0-367-19864-0 (pbk)
ISBN: 978-0-429-24378-3 (ebk)

Typeset in Bembo
by Cenveo® Publisher Services

Contents

Acknowledgements vi
Author Biographies viii

1. The Emergence of Computer Science in K–12 Schools 1
2. A Blueprint for Embedding Computer Science into Learning and Teaching 13
3. Abstraction 26
4. Algorithms 56
5. Programming 69
6. Data 92
7. Networks 107
8. Getting Started 124

Acknowledgements

We are grateful for the support of many colleagues, friends, and family who helped us throughout the writing of this book. We are indebted to Tony Picciano at the City University of New York, who fortuitously suggested to an editor at Routledge to talk with Tom about possible innovative directions the field might be going. That led Daniel Schwartz to meet with Tom and encourage the composition of this very book. So, Tony and Dan——thank you.

Tom would like to thank so many thought partners who have always been generous with their time and insights about K–12 computationality. To Michael Preston at the Joan Gantz Cooney Center; Daniel Rabuzzi, Founder of Indigo Pheasant LLC and Tom O'Connell of MOUSE.org; the education team at Sam Houston State University: Hannah Gerber, Tori Hollas, and Christina Ellis; Aankit Patel, formerly of the NYC Department of Education and now with the City University of NewYork; Britt Neuhaus at the Overdeck Family Foundation; Viraj Kamdar at The Bill & Melinda Gates Foundation; Amber Oliver at the Robin Hood Foundation; Jason Jefferies at Blenderbox; and dear friend, early musician, and CS guru Hank Heijink. To all of you: big ups.

Gerald learned how to teach CS to students thanks to the kindness and engagement of colleagues and students. He especially wants to thank Lauren Scollins, a terrific and passionate colleague. Gerald also wants to thank Frank Williams and Raymond Tribble of the White Plains New York Youth Bureau and Gerald Dennis of the Northeast Starter STEM Academy at Mt. Vernon (NSSA) for granting him the privilege of working with the young people in their programs. Gerald only hopes that these students learned half as much from him as he did from them.

For Pam, the journey towards integrating CS concepts in the ELA classroom has been an adventure filled with mutual respect from her two co-authors, Dr. Tom Liam Lynch and Dr. Gerald Ardito. She is humbled that they included her to be a part of this project and is inspired by their tireless efforts to create new knowledge. They have been a true delight to collaborate with on common interests in building new literacies with computer science concepts. To Dr. Christy Desmet, may she rest in peace, for cultivating Pam's love of Shakespeare. To Kristen Fowler, for encouraging Pam to extend her teaching practice outside her comfort zone. To Chris Michael for his brilliant computer science guidance. And, most importantly, Pam is eternally grateful for her soulmate John Amendola, who has been her biggest advocate and most ardent supporter. His compassion for others is Pam's inspiration to be a better human every day.

Author Biographies

Tom Liam Lynch is director of education policy at the Center for New York City Affairs at The New School and editor-in-chief of InsideSchools.org. A former educational technology professor, English teacher, and school district official for the New York City Department of Education, Tom led the implementation of a $50-million online learning program in over one hundred schools called iLearnNYC. He then architected and co-piloted the implementation of WeTeachNYC, a $6.8-million digital resource repository, learning environment, and blended learning program for the city's 80,000 teachers. Tom's research examines the relationship between software theory, literacy, and education reform. He has published widely and presented the world over on educational technologies, school reform, and new literacies. In 2019, Tom received the National Technology Leadership Initiative Award from the National Council of Teachers of English (NCTE) for his development of both theory and methods for embedding computer science in K–12 English classrooms. Learn more at tomliamlynch.com.

Gerald Ardito has been working in education for almost three decades. His experience includes adult education, adolescent biology, computer science, and, most recently, higher education. He is currently an associate professor of Computer Science Education at Manhattanville College, USA. He was previously a middle school science teacher and assistant professor of STEM-D education at Pace University, USA. His research interests include the development of self-directed, technology-enhanced learning environments and the development and deepening of computational thinking skills in K–12 students.

Author Biographies

Pam Amendola, EdS, has worked in education for seventeen years. Her experience includes teaching British and American literature, journalism, yearbook, and adult education. Prior to her current position at Dawson County High School in Dawsonville, Georgia, she had the pleasure of teaching many creative students at Brookwood High School. Her research interests include building literacy through computational thinking, creative use of AI in education, and transforming education for the Fourth Industrial Revolution.

The Emergence of Computer Science in K–12 Schools

We are tempted to assume that you think computer science is worth teaching in K–12 settings. After all, you have opened a book about that very topic. It would be safe to think that you need little convincing. But people open books like this for different reasons. Sure, you yourself might have an intrinsic interest in coding or robotics or things like that. It is also possible that someone else asked (or told) you to read this book. We get it. No judgement either way.

So, let's do this a little differently. Let's assume that you don't necessarily believe computer science has any place in K–12 schools. Let's assume that some readers might not even be sure what computer science means. A couple paragraphs into the first page, most readers are naturally skeptical—not sure they're 100 percent committed to the chapters that follow. To be fair, we, the authors, are skeptical about you, too. That's why we are going to level with you: We have little interest in computer science for its own sake. Not in this book.

Then why did we write it and why might it be worth your time? Give us a few more pages of your attention and we will explain.

We want to be transparent about why we believe we have a compulsory school system in the first place. In our experience, it is easy for teachers, parents, administrators, and elected officials to expound on the virtues or shortcomings of school without ever being clear about why schools are important. That is understandable when you realize that unlike most other nations to which we compare ourselves, the United States does not define the purpose of public education in the national Constitution. (No kidding. Google the Constitution and search around. You won't find words like *school* or *learning* or *teaching* or anything like that.) As a result, the purpose of our schools appears in state constitutions, but that means there are fifty different articulations of why we educate children.

Some articulations are specific and thoughtful, preparing children to participate in a democracy or contribute to an economy. Others are more problematic, like the many clauses in state constitutions that really don't say why educating children is important at all. They just say that states will use tax money to do it.

Here's why we believe we educate our children, and it is with this explicit purpose in mind that we frame our entire book. We argue that we have compulsory education in the United States because as a democratic republic, we rely on an informed population to participate in making our communities better. The individual right to vote does our nation little benefit if the individual is not taught to read, to write, to learn about the world, to assess the validity of arguments, and to engage in complex conversations with others about things that matter to us all. Tightly tethered to civic engagement is economic engagement. We educate our children because we want to know that they can contribute to our collective economy, whether it's holding down a steady job and providing for one's family or creating a new technology that changes the world. Civic and economic engagement—that is why we believe we have schools and that is also why we believe computer science must be meaningfully introduced into K–12 spaces.

Over the last twenty years, digital technologies have revolutionized the way so much of our society operates. First, there is the basic stuff most of us have begun to take for granted. We send messages to each other in an instant, share ideas and pictures, book tickets, and stream entertainment. Much of this happens on our phones or via ever-flattening computers. Second, there is the bigger stuff that happens digitally that we tend to think less about on a daily basis, like our banking systems, the entirety of the aviation industry, identification management, and medical record keeping. Digital technologies now mediate our individual and collective lives in ubiquitous, hidden, speedy, and wide-scaled ways.

With the spread of digital technologies has come new opportunities. In some parts of the world, you can order virtually any good or service you need from your phone and it will be provided in hours, if not minutes. You don't exchange money with the provider directly; it's all handled digitally. In other parts of the world, communities whose governments have not yet provided a basic communication infrastructure—either because they cannot or choose not to—can now access information via the Internet using very simple and inexpensive mobile phones. Digital technologies are credited with making democratic revolutions possible in countries like Egypt and Tunisia. The same technologies can make it possible for anybody, anywhere to learn something they need or want.

Digital technologies have become so much a part of our daily experience that we forget how little the average person really understands about how they work, who makes them work, and why. It was a lack of understanding that was put on full display in the wake of the 2016 presidential elections in the United States, when it became increasingly evident that social media platforms like Facebook and Twitter were used by foreign powers to stoke division among American voters. What's more, few understand just how much digital data are generated and collected about individuals today. Companies have been able to leverage more data than ever before in order to market to consumers. In many states, schools have also been encouraged to digitize more of their instructional and operational practices. There are mobile apps dedicated to classroom management and parental communication, web-based apps for running blended classrooms, and paper-based textbooks are on the decline. For administrators, grades are increasingly submitted via digital systems, student records are collected and shared via third-party products, and professional learning opportunities are increasingly offered and tracked online.

It all seems so normal. But how many readers know what data companies collect about our children and teachers and what they do with them? How many readers know how to spot a suspicious and inflammatory post in their social media feed? How many realize that when they share a picture online, they are sharing many dozen types of personal data with the company who owns the platform and device?

Our point is to say that today what it means to prepare young people for civic and economic engagement requires that they critically understand the way digital technologies enable and inhibit such engagement. Senior officials have warned of the danger of election systems being hacked throughout the world. But do our soon-to-be-voting children know what "hacking" an election consists of? Economic experts have foreshadowed that jobs across industries and pay scales will increasingly require at least a basic, if not an advanced, understanding of how to communicate with computers. But what happens when computer science as a subject is disproportionately offered to economically advantaged students or as a single elective or Advanced Placement course? We don't advocate computer science in K–12 schools and districts because it is in vogue or trendy. We advocate computer science in schools because we believe the future improvement of our society requires it. No hyperbole.

In our experience, there are two problems with K–12 computer science education in the United States. The first problem is *computer*. The second problem is *science*. Here's what we mean when we say that *computer* and *science* are so problematic:

1. **Computationality is not about "computers," per se. It is about inquiry, logic, and languages.** By overemphasizing the word "computer," advocates have deemphasized some important things about

digital technologies. First, you can learn about computationality without computers. Electricity isn't necessary. Second, computers don't appear out of the ether. Human beings build them, program them, and network them. Those human beings have different motivations for doing so, and any particular way they do it could always look differently than it does. We suggest forgetting about "computers" and think about computationality instead, including its distant etymological cousins *composition* and *communication*. When it comes down to it, computer science is fundamentally about systematically and logically communicating with machines—as well as how machines increasingly communicate with us (Frabetti, 2015). It is about how human beings compose instructions to tell machines what to do—and it is about realizing how computationality shapes the world around us. Once you realize that, you will begin to see that insofar as you and your students are fluent in communicating in any language, you already have the foundation to communicate with computers. It's all just inquiry and logic and language. At a talk in Seoul a few years ago, Tom told a group of several hundred English-language teachers that they in fact had comparable expertise in teaching coding in schools as computer science professors. Coding is just a form of writing, a way to communicate with a particular mechanical audience (Vee, 2017). Who better to help students learn to code than language teachers? There were a few claps, but most of the attendees remained unconvinced. But Tom meant it. Still does.

2. **Computationality is not about "science." It can deepen and expand learning in all grades and disciplines.** It might surprise you to know that the field of K–12 computer science is young compared with other subjects like secondary mathematics and English. In their eagerness to support schools in this important work, advocates sometimes treat computationality in an overly narrow way, limiting their paradigms to those of computer scientists and technology industry experts. The problems with the resultant paradigm are manifold. First, it means that computer science is framed as an external discipline that has to be introduced anew to existing K–12 school curricula and structures. But most schools already have a dense curriculum and tight schedules, and the traditional structures by which schools operate simply don't change swiftly. Ask a science or math teacher how much room in their curricula they have to include meaningful and extended activities in computer science. Watch them sweat. Second, and relatedly, by framing computer

science as a science, it means that non-STEM (science, technology, engineering, math) subjects are deemphasized as sites of computational study. And yet there are rich and engaging ways to embed computationality into the humanities, ways that deepen and expand disciplinary study. In short: forget computers and forget science. Think in terms of computationality. We believe that computational methods have a place across grades and disciplines and that embedding such methods into one's classroom can deepen and expand one's practice (Lynch, 2017).

Here's the paradox of K–12 computer science education: If you really believe that computer science is important for young people to learn, then it might be best to stop talking so much about computers and the sciences! Nevertheless, it is a familiar term and one we will use generously to refer to ways of thinking, solving problems, creating, and communicating that empower teachers and students to better understand how computers operate in the world. We will also use other terms at times, like *computational thinking*, *computationality*, and *computational methods*. In this book, those words are used mostly interchangeably. To better appreciate how computer science (see, we're back to using it already!) has been framed in schools currently, let's look at its emergence on the national stage in the United States and how the nation's largest school district attempted to introduce computer science to 1,800 schools at scale.

An Official, Top-Down Approach

In December 2014, President Barack Obama became the first president to write computer code as part of the White House's promotion of Computer Science Education Week and its Computer Science for All (CS4All) initiative (Finley, 2014). Nine months later, the nation's largest school district announced its plans to provide computer science education to its 1.1 million students and 80,000 teachers (Taylor & Miller, 2015). New York City might not be representative of many other districts, but nevertheless it serves as a case study for how computer science has emerged in American schools. Two main efforts took root in New York City to operationalize CS4All: a centralized and official top-down model and a decentralized and unofficial bottom-up model. The first effort was the city's establishment of a formal team in its central offices devoted to K–12 computer science education. The team focused on several ways to support schools, including: designing an accessible K–12 computer science framework for the city's teachers, soliciting sample curricula, and building community via social media.

Accessing K–12 Computer Science Frameworks

Multiple sets of K–12 computer science standards already exist. Two of the main ones in use are provided by the International Society for Technology in Education (ISTE) and another set created by the Computer Science Teachers Association (CSTA). The ISTE Computer Science Educator standards are divided into four areas: knowledge of [computer science] content, effective teaching and learning strategies, effective learning environments, and effective professional knowledge and skills. The CSTA standards (Seehorn et al., 2011) are somewhat more detailed and are organized into two areas: *concepts* and *practices*. Concepts include computing systems, networks and the Internet, data and analysis, algorithms and programming, and impacts of computing. Practices include fostering an inclusive computing culture, collaborating around computing, recognizing and defining computational problems, developing and using abstractions, creating computational artifacts, testing and refining computational artifacts, and communicating about computing. New York City's team felt that those two standards sets were aimed at teachers who taught computer science as an isolated content area. Their concern was that if computer science was going to be truly scaled in K–12 classrooms, there needed to be a framework for teachers across grade levels and content areas to integrate computational concepts and methods into the classes they were *already* teaching. (We should note that ISTE now also has a nimbler framework that they refer to as Computational Thinking Competencies.) So, New York City created their own framework, referring to the resultant document as the Blueprint. The Blueprint (New York City, n.d.) is divided into three main areas: perspectives, practices, and concepts. Perspectives frames learning via different roles students might play, which they call explorers, creators, innovators, and citizens. For practices, the team boiled it down to just three: analyzing, prototyping, and communicating. Finally, the core concepts the Blueprint puts forth are limited to abstraction, algorithms, programming, data, and networks. In each case, teachers can drill down on the website to see in greater detail what is meant by the various terms.

It is interesting to note that the team saw it necessary to design an entirely new heuristic when others existed already. Their rationale—that other standard sets like ISTE's and CSTA's were too focused on computer science as a separate subject—has proven a compelling one. Many public school districts lack the funding to sustain separate computer science teachers, courses, and programs. If officials truly want computer science for all students, then embedding computer science into current courses will likely be much more equitable and sustainable. To do that, an alternative framework like New York's seems reasonable.

Soliciting Sample Curricula

While drafting their Blueprint, the city's team began soliciting curricular samples from a wide array of partners. Tom and Gerald designed several. The city's goal was to amass a library of activities, projects, assignments, and units that 80,000 teachers could adapt or adopt for themselves. The units were aligned with instructional standards like the Common Core and, where possible, made explicit what computer science standards were being evoked. Interestingly, one of the challenges the team faced appeared to be within the city's own district offices. When Tom presented an assignment to the CS4All team in which students plotted word frequencies from Shakespeare, he was surprised to learn that the city's English Language Arts team would not approve it because it contained "too much English content." In short, the curricular team themselves did not appreciate just how innovative, strategic, and practical the CS4All team was being. What the CS4All team wanted was precisely what we argue is needed: teachers using computational methods to deepen and expand their content-area instruction. But what the curricular team wanted was a circumscribed computer science activity that wouldn't get in the way of teaching English. Still, the CS4All team persisted and ultimately made dozens of curricular resources available to the schools.

Building a Community via Social Media

A final tactic the team used to officially support schools was to build an ongoing conversation online via a weekly Twitter chat. Specifically, the team was interested in engaging teachers in some of the timely and knotty ethical questions that emerged for them when exploring computer science with minors. All under the hashtag #ethicalcs, the group posted questions and engaged in real-time discussion for an hour each week tackling issues like protecting student data and how information systems can perpetuate school segregation.

 # An Unofficial, Bottom-Up Approach

The second main effort to operationalize CS4All in New York City came through a nonprofit called Computer Science New York City (CSNYC). CSNYC was launched with the support of city and philanthropic funding. A core part of CSNYC's mission was to create an ecosystem for computer science education in the city. CSNYC became the premier connector of individuals and organizations doing work in New York City related to K–12 computer science. They established strategic partnerships, held meet-ups, sent out regular newsletters, and served as a constant reminder to others that there were many kinds of contributions one could make to the CS4All cause. Tom attended several of their events over the years. The range of curricular resources and services offered was often staggering, ranging from formalized nonprofits to impressive individual efforts. For example, MOUSE is a nonprofit that creates a variety of learning experiences for students who live in poverty and who are of color. MOUSE has a sizable workspace in downtown Manhattan where students come to learn about computing, robotics, electrical engineering, and more. Students might partner with an organization to learn about a pressing need and then design technological prototypes that attempt to solve the organization's problem. At the other end of the spectrum, take *Coding Train*. Started by Professor Daniel Shiffman, *Coding Train* is a YouTube channel in which Shiffman teaches anyone how to learn to code. With animations, a lively host, and ever-changing content, the channel has racked up nearly 750,000 subscribers, and the most popular videos have nearly 2 million views. Shiffman typically stands at his computer engaging with real-time comments or asynchronous requests. His backdrop is his screen, though, making the videos highly engaging. There were even other organizations teaching computational thinking through dance and gaming and Minecraft. The list was endless. Whereas the city's CS4All team offered official support to schools with a necessarily top-down feel to it, CSNYC worked from the ground up by becoming the force that connected all the smaller efforts that risked getting lost in the vastness of a city of 10 million people.

Nations and States Doing Their Own Thing

As we write this, national efforts to formally require K–12 computer science vary widely. Because education is mostly a state-controlled issue, it means that effecting change at scale requires fifty different state governments taking coordinated action. It just doesn't happen often. Some states are responding to grassroot calls from parents, schools, and the private sector to take computer science more seriously as a formal content area. New York, for instance, has a proposal on the books to certify computer science teachers at the K–12 level. As of 2018, twenty-two states had academic standards that framed K–12 computer science education. Fifteen states required high schools to make computer science an offered course. Thirty-three states had computer science teaching certification. And fourteen states had dedicated supervisors at the state level for computer science (Herold, 2018). In addition, the College Board revamped its Advanced Placement Computer Science course to de-emphasize narrow coding skills and underscore core computational principles and practices.

Again, what is essential to understand is that there is no one way K–12 computer science looks—certainly not nationally, not within individual states, and not within schools.

Compare what K–12 computer science looks like in the United States to what it looks like in other countries like the United Kingdom, Israel, and New Zealand. In those countries, as in most others, public education is administered nationally from a centralized office. The result is that when a country determines that computer science is a necessary subject for school-age children, they develop standards and implement the requirements nationwide. In 2016, Ireland had decided to make computer science compulsory in its schools. The education department conducted a landscape review of other countries that implemented computer science in schools nationally, including the countries named earlier. They found that despite tight administrative execution, those countries were not seeing an uptick in the number of young people going into computer science. Nor did they see the expected rise in women going into the field. When Tom gave a talk at Trinity College in Dublin that year, he suggested to the group that part of the reason multiple countries are all seeing the same result is—you guessed it—because they are teaching computer science too narrowly. Rather than just thinking about computer science as a separate subject, countries also needed to acknowledge computational methods as applicable to all content areas. Do that and you might see different results. A rich discussion ensued, with professors from education and computer science weighing in. Ultimately, though, the Irish government proceeded to go about compulsory computer science the same way other nations did. The results are predictable.

In the United States, the decentralized nature of our national school system is a blessing and a curse. It is a blessing because, if other nations' approaches are representative, we are avoiding going down a very disappointing road where great funding is earmarked for something that doesn't ultimately manifest. However, the curse is that it means there is no "right" way to implement computer science in K–12 settings. That can be liberating for some schools and daunting for others. There are many ways to do this work, limited only by one's creativity and resources (strictly in that order), and there are other, more research-driven books that might complement the practices discussed here (Kafai & Burke, 2014; Margolis, Estrella, Goode, Holme, & Nao, 2008; Resnick, 2017). In the chapters that follow, we will share with you some of our insights on what we have done and what we might do differently in the future. Both Tom and Gerald are education professors with expertise in technology in schools. Pam is a high school English teacher in Georgia with some informal background in computer science. Together, we hope to share stories from our experiences that reveal insights and principles of practice that can be applied systematically in your classroom, school, or district. Here's a breakdown of what to expect.

How to Read the Book

This is Chapter 1, where we frame what we mean by computer science, assert some beliefs about K–12 computer science education, offer some background context, and set the tone for the rest of the book. In Chapter 2, we offer a closer look at New York City's Blueprint, which we have found to be extraordinarily helpful in providing not only a heuristic but also concrete actionable resources for teachers across grades and content areas. In Chapter 3, we begin our focus on key computational concepts, starting with abstraction. In it, Gerald walks us through a story about how he used circuit boards to teach life science. Next, in Chapter 4, Tom takes you into a crowded cafeteria where hundreds of elementary students participate a Rock, Paper, Scissors tournament in order to uncover what algorithms are all about. In Chapter 5, Gerald demystifies programming with his stories about middle schoolers, robots, and collaborative learning. Tom returns in Chapter 6 to share his project in which students use quantitative data about literature—specifically, word frequencies—to deepen their experiences with reading. Chapter 7 pulls us into Pam's classroom, where she works with her students to teach Shakespeare through robotics. Let us say that again: Shakespeare through robotics. And finally, we conclude in Chapter 8 with a toolkit for getting started in your own settings. It's a chapter loaded with straight advice and tools you can use immediately.

While you can jump around in the book, we recommend reading the chapters in order. It might be tempting for a content-area teacher to want to skip chapters that don't appear to focus on their preferred discipline, but we would discourage you from doing so. There is so much to learn from the work that happens across grades and content areas. What's more, we make sure that the chapters framed around concepts actually always give examples of what it might look like across disciplines. The principles of practice that emerge from different chapters can always—always—be adapted for grades and content areas other than the specific ones illustrated. You will get the most out of the book by reading each chapter in order and always translating for your own setting what can be adopted and adapted.

 ## Conclusion

Bringing K–12 computer science to your classroom, school, and district is uncharted territory, but that is not to say it is unexplored. You can see that whether you look at how it plays out in different schools, how different states are attempting to respond to growing demand, or how other countries implement national programs. There is no one way to do it. We think that with such openness comes phenomenal potential to create K–12 computer science models that are truly responsive to the needs of each individual community. As you prepare to learn more from our experiences, remember the two key points made earlier:

1. Computer science is not a STEM subject. It can deepen and expand learning in all grades and disciplines.
2. Computer science is more than a technical subject. It's about inquiry, logic, and language.

With that in mind, let's begin exploring core computational concepts, beginning with New York City's Blueprint.

References

Finley, K. (2014, December 8). Obama becomes first president to write a computer program. Retrieved March 22, 2015, from https://www.wired.com/2014/12/obama-becomes-first-president-write-computer-program/

Frabetti, F. (2015). *Software theory: A cultural and philosophical study.* New York: Rowan & Littlefield Education.

Google, Inc., & Gallup, Inc. (2016). Trends in the state of computer science in US K–12 schools. Retrieved from http://services.google.com/fh/files/misc/trends-in-the-state-of-computer-science-report.pdf

Herold, Benjamin. "States Aggressively Adopting K–12 Computer Science Policies, Report Finds." *Education Week*, 8 Oct. 2018, https://blogs.edweek.org/edweek/DigitalEducation/2018/10/states_adopting_k-12_computer_science_policy.html.

Kafai, Y. B., & Burke, Q. (2014). *Connected code: Why children need to learn programming*. Cambridge, MA: MIT Press.

Lynch, T. L. (2017). How English teachers will save the future: Re-imagining computer science as the language art it is. *STEM Journal, 18*(4), 163–180.

Margolis, J., Estrella, R., Goode, J., Holme, J. J., & Nao, K. (2008). *Stuck in the shallow end: Education, race, and computing*. Cambridge, MA: MIT Press.

New York City Department of Education. "What Is CS Education?" *CS4All NYC*, n.d., http://blueprint.cs4all.nyc/what-is-cs/.

Resnick, M. (2017). *Lifelong kindergarten: Cultivating creativity through projects, passion, peers, and play*. Cambridge, MA: MIT Press.

Seehorn, D., Carey, S., Fuschetto, B., Lee, I., Moix, D., O'Grady-Cunniff, D., … Verno, A. (2011). CSTA K-12 Computer Science Standards. Retrieved January 14, 2016, from https://csta.acm.org/Curriculum/sub/CurrFiles/CSTA_K-12_CSS.pdf

Taylor, K., & Miller, C. C. (2015, September 15). De Blasio to announce a 10-year deadline to offer computer science to all students. *New York Times*. Retrieved from http://www.nytimes.com/2015/09/16/nyregion/de-blasio-to-announce-10-year-deadline-to-offer-computer-science-to-all-students.html?_r=0

Vee, A. (2017). *Coding literacy: How computer programming is changing writing*. Cambridge, MA: MIT Press.

A Blueprint for Embedding Computer Science into Learning and Teaching

It was Texas. And it was summer. Now, hot is one thing. But hot in Texas with a dubious air conditioner at a mostly empty high school building is something else altogether. A team from a public university was preparing to welcome nearly one hundred pre-service teachers to a week-long training in computational thinking that would culminate the following week with teachers running a camp for 300 elementary, middle, and high school students. As they prepared for the teachers' arrival in a large group instructional room, it was clear that the heat was going to be an issue. In a moment of insight, the team decided to pull the temporary wall from its closet in order to divide the room in two. One hundred teachers crammed into half the space, but with twice the cold air. As teachers took their seats, it was clear that everyone was slightly closer to their neighbors than they'd like.

Addressing the group, Tom and his collaborator Dr. Hannah R. Gerber of Sam Houston State University suggested everyone look around them and move their tables a little up or down or left or right—wherever they had some additional room. Within a few minutes, the group was breathing a little easier.

"This week-long workshop can be summed up in what we just did. We saw a problem. We identified what steps we could take to fix it. Then we systematically acted on those steps in order to create a better situation. That's computational thinking in a nutshell," Tom concluded.

Participants looked around the room. Some were excited. Others showed signs of regret, the sort of hopelessness one might observe of queasy guests on a ship that just left the dock. The journey ahead might be promising, but it wasn't clear that its promise could outweigh the humidity of Houston.

As the conversation with the group continued, there were persistent and recurring barriers to teachers feeling comfortable exploring computer science. First, they were intimidated or confused by the terminology that comprises the field. Words like *algorithm* or *programming* can intimidate the average teacher. Second, many participants appeared skeptical that computer science was really something they needed to spend their precious time exploring. After all, it's not like the state was assessing computer science, so it ultimately felt like a nice-to-have but hardly something that teachers should be spending their summers learning about. Finally, computer science sounded like its own confident field—which it is—so it was hardly clear how it relates with other content areas. Put it all together and you have a room of overheated teachers whose attention was due more to politeness than to interest.

We will share more about that professional learning experience in the chapters ahead. What is most important at this point is to understand what happened next. In looking at the participants, who were sweating and crammed and slowly cooling off, Tom continued.

"As we begin this work this week, I need you to understand one thing: No one knows how best to teach K–12 computer science. There are lots of approaches, but many of them are informed by big technology companies or computer science professors. Don't get me wrong. They are all well-intentioned and some are useful. But they tend to come from outside K–12 schooling and attempt to push computer science into classrooms. We think about this work differently. We start with the curriculum and instruction already underway in your school, looking for strategic ways to use computationality to deepen and expand that work."

Participants exchanged glances. Their expressions appeared to say, "So, why do we have to learn any of this?"

"The reason to care and to concentrate on computational thinking this week is as follows. There is more computing power in the smartphone in your pocket than NASA had for the Apollo missions. That technology is mediating more and more of what we do as a society: how we find dinner, how we find love, how we vote, how we find the news, how we plan a wedding, how we find an attorney when the marriage doesn't work out, how we find a doctor, and how we find a funeral home. In the same way that reading and writing has always been a priority in learning and teaching, the twenty-first century demands that we also understand how to read and write with and through computationality—computer science."

As suggested in Chapter 1, if you are like many people, you don't necessarily identify with the word "computer" or even perhaps "science." In looking for a place to start, you might find yourself searching the wilds of the Internet in hopes of unearthing some comprehensive document that clarifies for you what to do. Recall that there are many to choose from, with the options seeming to increase each month. A popular first find is a standard set created by the Computer Science Teachers Association (CSTA).

If your school has formal computer science classes, then few other resources can rival the thoroughness one finds in its pages. Another oft-cited series of competencies comes from the International Society for Technology in Education (ISTE). ISTE has developed international influence in the educational technology space over the years. They provide guidelines for both computer science educators and broader competencies intended for a wide range of teachers. Even Google—yes, the very Google you might have used to find the CSTA or ISTE standards—has its model for teaching computer science, which is part of its CS First initiative.

There is value in each of these frameworks and others that your school or district might encounter. And after you feel more comfortable with what embedding computer science in your practice might look like, we encourage you to see what they have to offer. But these are not the frameworks we recommend beginning with. The thoroughness of the CSTA standards, for instance, will quickly overwhelm most people who do not have formal computer science training. If your school is focused on embedding computational thinking rather than teaching a formal computer science course, then the CSTA standards might be overkill. You'll stop before you start. Other standards might strike school leaders or teaching teams as too vague—conceptually useful but operationally thin.

As briefly mentioned in the previous chapter, our preferred framework for understanding computer science as it relates to K–12 settings comes by way of the New York City Department of Education. It just so happens that the city that never sleeps really burned the midnight oil to create something incredibly valuable to educators the world over. Understanding that making computer science available for all meant embedding computer science across grade levels and content areas, the city's CS4All team designed a "Blueprint" for computer science that offers a smart, elegant, and nimble framework for any school or district. It's so thoughtful that we restructured this book after some initial feedback from reviewers, realizing that we did not need to invent a new heuristic. New York did a stellar job. (Note: We will refer often to the Blueprint, quoting from it throughout the book. You can find everything you need to know about it by visiting https://blueprint.cs4all.nyc/what-is-cs/)

The Blueprint is broken up into several components that provide educators multiple entry points into thinking about how best to embed computer science into their practice. First, it describes computer science perspectives. Perspectives refer to the ways in which educators envision their students identifying as they explore computer science. Or, put more succinctly, "Meaningful computer science units help students fully embrace a *perspective* such that they are ready and interested in progressing to the next" (italics added). Four main perspectives are described in the Blueprint, each of which will be discussed further: explorer, creator, innovator, and citizen. Second, the Blueprint describes three high-level practices that subsume groups of key skills. The core practices are analyzing, prototyping, and communicating. Finally, the creators of the Blueprint suggest five core computer science concepts that can guide one's pedagogy: abstraction, algorithms, programming, data, and networks. When combined, the Blueprint provides the contours for teachers' curriculum and instruction in a manner that honors the uniqueness of both the traditional content areas and computer science. They even weave the components together into a student outcome matrix, specific enough to be meaningful but flexible enough to be useful.

Now, before we dive into each of the components a bit further, we want to acknowledge that some readers might find these terms intimidating. That's OK. You actually know way more about all this than you think you do. We suspect that after the next several pages, you will begin to appreciate just how accessible much of this is. With that being said, let's dive into it.

Perspectives

There are many ways for students and teachers to encounter computational methods. Most of us are simply users, meaning we have embraced some aspect of digital technologies in our lives for fun or functional purposes, but we do not think about it much further. We check email. We text with family. We might even post to social media. We binge-watch old television series. But not much more. As you start to consider what it means to teach computer science in your school or district, you will want to shake things up.

All these digital technologies we experience, they are created by teams of people somewhere. Created. That means, just like we would never accept teaching children (or ourselves) to read without also learning to write, we want to demystify how to produce the kinds of phenomena we heretofore only consumed. The Blueprint argues for four personas to help us do so: one who *explores* computer science, one who *creates* with computational methods, one who *innovates* through computationality, and one who uses what one knows about computationality to help improve their community *civically*. The final emphasis on the role of being civically engaged is, for us, a powerful perspective. Recall that we advocate computer science in K–12 schools not because it's in vogue or because we think it will prepare children for jobs or because parents are screaming for it. The primary reason to teach it is because many crucial aspects of society are increasingly mediated by digital technologies. The citizen perspective in the Blueprint offers a way to take with seriousness the civic impetus.

Explorer

When students are explorers, they are focused on playing with computational concepts and practices in focused and flexible ways. They might program a robot to do a simple maneuver or learn how to draw a design using variables. As the Blueprint states, "The goal of this exploration is to help students build familiarity and facility with CS so they can progress to becoming creators who are able to start defining the ideas they would like to express through CS." Importantly, such activities can be used in elementary school as the bulk of the learning experiences, or they can be used in middle and high school settings as introductions to deeper work. But remember, especially at the secondary level, the goal is to embed computational methods in ways that ultimately deepen and expand the content area. It is not enough to have a CS day in one's classroom that only glibly relates to the disciplinary heart and soul of the curriculum. Maybe start there, but don't mistake it for the goal.

Creator

After students become more comfortable with computational concepts and methods, the next step is to help them "use friendly, open-ended physical and digital tools to represent their ideas, thoughts, or interests." Whereas a student with the explorer perspective might modify some existing simple computer code to make a robot do the hokey pokey, a student in a creator mind set envisions a more authentic problem or purpose for which computationality can help. For instance, a student might better understand the tactful errors of Napoleon's Waterloo by programming robots to reenact the battle. Or a student might wish to use data gathered from probes in science class to create a series of visualizations that shows pH levels in water supplies. What drives the creator perspective is a newfound sense of fluency with computational concepts and methods that makes posing real questions and making new solutions possible.

Innovator

To be an innovator is to "build and share ideas, thoughts, and interests with others by contributing to or building on other projects." There is a deep sense that the work one does necessarily interrelates with the work of others. Remember that digital technologies are all powered by software and that software is composed of

Blueprint for Embedding Computer Science

lots of different computational languages written by different people at different times for different discrete purposes. There would be no Digital Age without the contributions of others. No lone coder hiding in the shadows of his dorm room—let's make that *her* dorm room, thank you very much—was ever going to code the Internet. The innovator perspective requires that students situate their own creativity and explorations in the context of others. Computationality comes from a collective effort, and it should ultimately contribute to a collective need. The Blueprint gives the example of a student who creates an interactive map "showing average temperature by year in a website that she created to discuss the impacts of humans on the environment." In short, the student used the programming languages and tools created by others to herself create something that contributed to solving others' problems. That's innovation.

Citizen

At first glance, the word "citizen" might seem unrelated to computer science in K–12 schools. We also acknowledge that in some communities, citizenship has become a complex topic and can be both a point of hope and fear for families, students, and teachers. Not all children or parents are officially citizens. Depending on where one lives at a given time, not being a citizen can make one the target of formal and informal investigations, harassment, or worse. In the way the word is used in the Blueprint, "citizen" refers to the broader notion of students being civically minded. Unfortunately, there isn't a clear pithy word in English to convey "someone who demonstrates civic-mindedness" other than citizen. As suggested in Chapter 1, the notion of civic engagement is actually vital to understanding why schools and districts should bother with computer science in the first place. Recall that one of the reasons we like the Blueprint as a framework for approaching computer science in K–12 schools and districts is because we believe that the ultimate purpose of a K–12 school system is to prepare young people to contribute to society in productive ways, to be politically, economically, and socially generous with their time and talents. The citizen perspective attempts to capture that ultimate purpose. The Blueprint gives examples like students writing to other students to encourage them to better address issues like fake news, students debating the ethical issues of self-driving cars, and a student who designed a more equitable algorithm for the way students are placed in schools in New York City. (Unlike most other districts, where students go to elementary, middle, and high school in the Big Apple is not determined on geographic location alone. Instead, all families have to apply for schools or be placed in a school based on the city's own criteria and algorithmic logic.) To be computationally savvy and civically engaged is the ultimate end for the Blueprint authors. The authors of this book agree.

 ## Practices

A natural next question to ask is what kinds of things students are expected to do while donning the roles of an explorer or creator or innovator or citizen. Perspectives are helpful, but what skills are students learning? That's where practices come in. The Blueprint team identified three high-level practices that each contain a series of discrete skills. You will notice that the skills they describe below are not unique to computer science. Not at all. They are the kinds of skills one would expect to hear teachers talking about in any grade or content area. You already know them. As you read, it's helpful to understand that the Blueprint team presents them in sequential order based on Webb's Depth of Knowledge, a popular instrument used internationally for ensuring rigorous curriculum and instruction. Though we won't go into significant depth with the practices, let's gain a working familiarity with each.

Analyzing

When students analyze something, they are expected to engage in a process of critically understanding how a particular phenomenon operates. They might begin by describing what they see, like the way users interact with a mobile app on their phone. Then students might examine their *description* of the app and identify ways that the different parts of the design affect how it is used. After *examining* their description, students might *interpret* what they observed and make an *evaluation* that results in recommending changes in colors or buttons or layouts to make the app easier to use for Luddites like us. The point is that when students analyze, they are focused on the systematic observation of how something works in the world—keeping in mind the potential to make it better.

Prototyping

If analyzing is about systematically defining a problem, prototyping is about designing a potential solution. Let's stick with that example of a mobile app that befuddles people like us. Once an evaluation is in hand, students might begin the process of building a solution or a prototype. First, students might *iterate* some different features that could fix different shortcomings of the app. Next, students might *imagine* a sweeping overhaul of the app that improves its ease of use. Then, students might *plan* in detail all the specific changes they could make, ultimately *designing* a comprehensive overhaul of the app. The stages to prototyping overlap in some ways and can complement other popular approaches in some schools, like design thinking and project-based learning. Ultimately, the focus of prototyping is about students engaging with concrete problems and detailed solutions.

Communicating

Like all forms of learning, computer science requires students to be able to communicate their work to others in a range of different contexts. One might begin by *showing* what one is wondering or creating, a relatively simple step that requires, for some students (and adults, mind you), a leap of confidence and faith. As a student shows others what she has created, the next step is to *explain* why she made what she made and how it works. Both showing and explaining can be done relatively informally, but to *present* one's work—even in a small setting—often takes on a bit more of a formal tone. Ultimately, the hope is that students can arrive at a place where they are comfortable discussing both the product of their creativity and the process they underwent to bring it to fruition.

 ## Concepts

Up to now, we suspect that the categories and skills presented in the Blueprint are mostly quite familiar to you. Some of the examples might refer to digital technologies or software, but not in an overly disorienting way. That's a real strength of the Blueprint: two-thirds of it is rooted in things educators already know or do or value. The final component is called concepts. This is where some educators might start to feel out of their element. But as with much of what we just surveyed, you actually know far more than you think you do. Like, way more. In our experience, it's the terms that freak people out—abstraction, algorithms, programming, data, and networks—because they appear to belong to an elite group in society whom we might call software engineers or computer scientists or programmers.

But those terms we just listed, and many more, do not belong to them or anyone else. We believe that last sentence so passionately. If we can just help you see that these terms that feel so far from your daily world are actually a part of your experiences in and out of schools, we know that your entire paradigm as it relates to computer science will shift. Almost in an instant.

Here's what we are going to do. We are going to provide a brief overview of the five main concepts framed in the Blueprint. You will get an accessible definition that alludes to real-life examples of the concept in both digital and analogue (nondigital) forms. Then, because we know that becoming confident in what these concepts are and look like in educational settings is the lynchpin that will enable you to make computer science a meaningful part of your classroom, school, or district, we are going to devote an entire chapter to each of the concepts so you can really see what they are all about. But wait. If the idea of reading a chapter about algorithms is not appealing, we encourage you to stay with us. Trust that what you think you already know or don't know about algorithms is probably incomplete. Trust that you know more than you think. And trust that computationality isn't an end in itself—not in this book. Computationality has the potential to deepen and expand your current classroom practice, to take it to exciting new places for your students, yes, but even more importantly: for you. In we go.

Abstraction

Life is complex. Sometimes, when we encounter too much complexity, it can be helpful to describe something in broader terms. Ever overhear someone explain something to someone else by saying, "Don't overthink it. It's like. . ."? To say one thing is like another thing is to drift into the realm of abstraction. The Blueprint team describes abstraction as follows: "An abstraction represents a simplified idea or problem derived by ignoring details and using patterns or general characteristics." We will explore this further in Chapter 3.

Algorithms

If you have ever cooked with a recipe, then you have experienced an algorithm. The Blueprint team defines algorithms as "a generalized and repeatable sequence of instructions that achieve a particular purpose and output, given a set of inputs.

Blueprint for Embedding Computer Science

It's important to understand when, why and how to implement an algorithm, and to consider who or what might be affected." In the background of everyday life, computers are following instructions about how to collect, process, and act on information. It's why you get the ads you do on your phone, for example. Chapter 4 will be devoted to this intimidating term that is, in so many ways, very familiar.

Programming

Cue the flashing images of dimly lit dorm rooms with aloof and lonely coders hunched over their laptops protected from the world only by their audacity and hoodies. That's not really what programming is. Programming refers to the writing of computer code in order to tell computers what you want them to do. The Blueprint describes programming as "giving instructions to computers. Programming can be done through a constantly changing set of languages." Remember in Chapter 1 we tried to emphasize that software is composed of languages, that when we speak of anything that is "digital," we are speaking about human and computational languages. Well, programming is the broad term used to capture that. In Chapter 5, we will demystify programming further.

Data

Data just refers to information that can be collected, stored, retrieved, and manipulated by human beings and computers. That's all. Some refer to data in the Digital Age as being "big". That's fair. The amount of data being collected and shared and used today is unimaginable. We will say more about the complexity of digital data in Chapter 6. There, we will explore the Blueprint team's definition in greater depth, which reads: "Computers can be used to collect, store and analyze massive amounts of data quickly and reliably. Computer programs can use data to make decisions or to automate tasks."

Networks

The fact that the Internet works at all is borderline miraculous. It is, fundamentally, just a collection of computers talking to each other really quickly in ways that would strike the average person as gibberish. All the digital devices we have in our lives work because of that interconnectedness. Or to put it differently, networks. The Blueprint uses the Internet as their main example as well (though others exist) when they write, "Networks, like the Internet, allow computers to interface with other computers through a set of rules, or protocols, that define how computers send and receive data. Protocols and standards are created and agreed upon by groups of people." Understanding networks is a key component of being able to critically explore computationality in our world, to which we will devote Chapter 7.

There is one more thing to know about the computational concepts described earlier. While they appear to be distinct, they seldom are. That is, you can certainly explore them individually but when it comes to real-life experience and practice, they often overlap. Take *Minecraft* as an example. *Minecraft* is a popular first-person point-of-view video game in which players explore a virtual world while accumulating supplies that help them build their own worlds. When you watch someone play *Minecraft*, it is hard to pry apart the various computational concepts. First, a virtual world is, by its nature, an abstraction. It is an immersive environment meant to emulate key aspects of our own lives. Algorithms operate in the background in order to present players with hints or resources needed. But beyond that, players get to create their own buildings by following step-by-step instructions that they either create or that they learn about via fan blogs. Once players master the basics, they can program their own customizations into their *Minecraft* worlds. Throughout this process, players are constantly receiving and acting on data provided, like health, mapping, and more. Finally, while *Minecraft* can be played on a discrete gaming console, the fun of it is when one enters into one of the myriad networked worlds available. A player in Texas can literally (well, digitally so) enter into the virtual world of a *Minecraft* player in Thailand.

The point of this example is to drive home the idea that computational concepts often—if not always—intertwine. They can be introduced and explored separately, but doing so is somewhat artificial. It would be like identifying the distinct notes in a chord: helpful for analysis and understanding, but it misses the real beauty of the thing.

 ## Back in Texas, Conceptually

North of Houston, teachers at the professional development sessions had made a daily point of identifying the culinary experiences Tom, as a New Yorker, needed to have while in the Lone Star State. There were some eateries Tom had heard about back East, like Sonic and Chick-fil-A. Those were known in Manhattan, but hardly ubiquitous. However, a particular hamburger joint emerged as near and dear to the participants and thoroughly unavailable back home. It was called Whataburger. Not, as Tom originally believed, Waterburger or even Whadaburger. Those were amateurish misnomers that would have proved the lie to any local with whom Tom spoke.

He needed to know what Whataburger was all about.

Tom punched into his phone's mapping application the name of the location. The nearest Whataburger was a mere two and a half miles away. Before he knew it, he was in his rented car, cold air blasting, sunglasses on, and Garth Brooks crooning in the background. When he put the car in reverse to leave the hotel parking lot, a rearview camera shot appeared on the screen on his dashboard. It superimposed green, yellow, and red lines onto the view to show how near or far the vehicle was from danger. The voice of artificial intelligence guided him out of the parking lot and on to the highway. Surprisingly at first, then comfortingly, a subtle orange light glowed on the interior opposite the sideview mirrors, sensors alerting him that another car was moving through his blind spot.

It took seven minutes to get to Whataburger.

He ordered his burger, paid by wanding his phone over a credit card scanner, and sat to enjoy a triple hamburger with bacon, avocado, mustard, mayo, and no bun. Bite by bite, Tom streamed through his social media feed to see teachers talking about the day's workshops on Twitter. They would soon be full-time educators, responsible for the lives of individual children, yes, but more than that. Every teacher has the potential to affect the trajectory of a child, which in and of itself is a powerful effect. But more so, every student that teachers affect has the potential to redirect the trajectory of entire families for generations.

That's what happened in Tom's family. He and his sisters were the first ones to go from high school to college. After that, it became a norm for other members of the family to do the same. For every teacher who demystifies computationality, dozens of families acquire the potential to participate in society in radically different ways than we currently imagine. The burger was delightful. And with each like, retweet, and comment he saw from his Houstonian pedagogues, Tom mused just how necessary computer science was becoming to life, even if one didn't yet realize it. Without it, you couldn't find a Whataburger, back out of a parking lot, navigate to a fast food spot, listen to your tunes, and appreciate the passion and authenticity of a whole new crew of teachers. In order to ensure that future teachers possessed a critical and creative understanding of the place of computationality in the world, what was needed was a new way of engaging with core computational concepts. And that, we are happy to say, is what comes next for you.

 ## For Further Exploration

- Read | CSTA Standards: https://www.csteachers.org/page/standards
- Read | ISTE Standards: https://www.iste.org/standards/computational-thinking
- Explore | CS First: https://csfirst-beta.withgoogle.com/s/en/home
- Study | Blueprint: https://blueprint.cs4all.nyc/what-is-cs/

3 Abstraction

One Thanksgiving not too long ago, Tom joined his in-laws for the annual tradition of converging at his wife's childhood home. The house sits on a few acres of land a couple hours north of Manhattan. The trees at that time of year turn glorious shades of red and orange and yellow. Wafting in the air are classic holiday scents: turkey, butter, cinnamon, sweet potatoes, cookies, and cakes. This particular year, Tom added to the victuals his own contribution in the form of a fine bottle of wine. For reasons that will be clear shortly, he does not remember its exact vintage or varietal or vineyard. He imagines it was probably a medium-bodied red wine from either the Loire Valley in France or from right there in the Hudson Valley.

Not too long before midnight, Tom excitedly burst into the kitchen with his smartphone in hand. The bottle had been opened a few hours earlier, not thoroughly shared in the spirit of the holiday or family, but not hoarded either. (Not intentionally, anyway.) He showed his wife and mother-in-law the screen of his phone. It had a picture of a chessboard on it. The button below the picture featured one word: Buy! Tom's wife, Kerry, quickly pointed out the price of the board. Conveniently, Tom doesn't remember exactly how much it cost. But it is safe to say it cost over $300. In what might well have been a defining moment in their marriage, Kerry looked at the excitement on Tom's face, the cost of the board, the empty bottle of wine, and the time on the clock.

"If it will make you happy, go ahead."

It would be false to call Kerry's tone truly supportive or encouraging. Rather, it was said with an experienced appreciation for which battles are worth fighting and which ones are unwinnable in the moment.

Buy Tom did.

Abstraction

We will return to this event throughout the next few chapters as a way to build your understanding of the concepts under exploration. Our first concept is abstraction.

The Blueprint says that abstraction "represents a simplified idea or problem derived by ignoring details and using patterns or general characteristics." Chess itself is an abstraction. A chessboard is an eight by eight grid that features sixteen pieces per side: a queen, a king, two bishops, two knights, two rooks (castle-looking things), and eight pawns. The two warring sides must use their respective pieces, each of which has unique movement abilities and limitations, to put the king in checkmate. The side that does so first wins.

When you play chess, you are not actually battling the other person. There are no real kings or queens or armies. The board, pieces, and rules are all abstractions. Thousands of years ago, someone had the idea to extract certain key components of warfare and turn them into a game that could be played to help train others on military strategy. At its core, that is all abstraction is. Abstraction is all around you. Time is an abstraction. Language is an abstraction. The pictures you see on whatever screen is in front of you are abstractions. You already know what abstraction is. What you don't perhaps know so clearly is what abstraction means in a computational context, but a classroom illustration is all that's needed to take care of that.

The Science of Turtles and Squares

When Gerald was a middle school life science teacher, he designed a project for his seventh-grade students. One of the key concepts of his life science curriculum was *feedback mechanisms*: the process by which living organisms and living systems respond to changes in their internal and external environments. Gerald believed that this was an excellent concept to explore through computationality. He believed that embedding computer science (CS) and computational thinking (CT) skills, practices, and projects into existing content areas could be a meaningful way to deepen and expand his students' experience of science. Specifically, he wanted his seventh-grade students to program interactive machines using the Arduino microprocessor, making connections between the notion of feedback in the worlds of computationality and nature.

This project focused on a key concept of science—feedback mechanisms—and was to be accomplished through the students' use of coding tools. Realizing these differences between the science concepts and his students' limited previous experience with coding, along with the likely challenges and the corresponding levels of abstraction required, Gerald designed his coding program accordingly. His plan was to support his students by managing levels of abstraction, increasing and decreasing, throughout this six-week experience.

Gerald's students, at the point in the school year when they were about to engage in this project, had already had several experiences with feedback mechanisms through their study of science. They had learned the relationships between photosynthesis (where plants transform carbon dioxide into energy in the form of glucose) and cellular respiration (where glucose is broken down to release the energy stored in it). They had investigated food chains and food webs to see that a complex system can respond to some degree of change, but that other degrees of change are too severe to survive.

In his project entitled *Introduction to the Feedback Mechanism*, Gerald challenged students to program an interactive device using the Arduino microprocessor. The project consisted of four parts: 1) Block-based coding in Turtle Blocks, 2) designing and coding an interactive device in Python Turtle, 3) text-based coding in Arduino, and 4) exhibiting and reflecting. Let's take a closer look.

At the outset, Gerald demonstrated examples of interactive devices for students to see in order to generate some excitement. During block-based coding, students learned to code with Turtle Blocks, a platform for block-based graphical programming. Students participated in a series of coding challenges that would allow them to build core CS skills, which they would then be able to translate into text-based coding later. Students then transitioned from block-based to text-based coding in designing and coding an interactive device in Python Turtle. In this phase, students used Python's Turtle library to translate the work they did with blocks in Turtle Blocks into text in the popular coding language Python. Then, as they engaged with text-based coding in Arduino, students were introduced to the Arduino board, electronic circuits, and the Arduino software integrated development environment (IDE). Lastly, during exhibition and reflection, students shared their work with their peers and then had a chance to reflect on what they had learned. This reflection focused on the obstacles students encountered and the work they did to overcome them.

Gerald designed the multiphased project with two key elements in mind. The first was that in each phase, students were presented with challenges that were to be met. These challenges featured clear goals, but had many possible solutions, allowing for student exploration and autonomy. The second key element was that each phase transferred skills from one programming language to another. For example, students learned to draw shapes with Turtle Blocks, then learned to

Abstraction

accomplish the same task in Python. This project took place over six weeks, with students doing the work during most of their scheduled science class time.

Let's look at each phase of the project in more detail.

Phase 1: Block-Based Coding with Turtle Blocks

Turtle Blocks is a block-based coding tool. It was designed by Sugar Labs, which developed the operating system and software for the One Laptop Per Child (OLPC) XO Laptops. As with the popular introductory coding language Scratch (see Chapter 5), users create programs by snapping digital blocks together. Turtle Blocks differs from Scratch in that it is focused on creating artwork, whereas Scratch is centered on animating characters called sprites (at least at the beginning). In this phase of Gerald's project, the students were presented with a series of challenges that provide them with an opportunity to master core CS skills.

In Turtle Blocks, Gerald began by having students create a program to draw basic shapes. In this case, students were challenged to create a program in Turtle Blocks that instructs the turtle to draw a square (see Figure 3.1).

This is only the first challenge in a series. Once they can draw a square, students are challenged to change the color of each side of the square. Squares are concrete, colors slightly less so. This challenge introduces more programming blocks to the student, in this case, the "set color" block. Students also learn that colors are represented as numbers, as are other properties in Turtle Blocks and other computing languages. Colors represented as numbers? See how far we are now from the concreteness of a simple square (see Figure 3.2.).

Next, students work to draw squares that have a different color on each side, and then to create a program that draws a square with randomly selected colors on each side. Alternating colors add yet another level of abstraction. This challenge introduces the blocks controlling numbers, which include randomly generated quantities. Randomly generated numbers is a slightly more abstract concept than just numbers representing colors. The students also learn that since colors are represented as numbers in Turtle Blocks, randomly generated numbers will change the color of each side (see Figure 3.3.).

Gerald then challenged his class to find the simplest way to have more than one turtle draw a square with a randomly generated color on each side. While they can certainly accomplish this challenge by having each new turtle have the same code they have already created, they soon realize that this gets cumbersome to both create and maintain this code as they add more and more turtles.

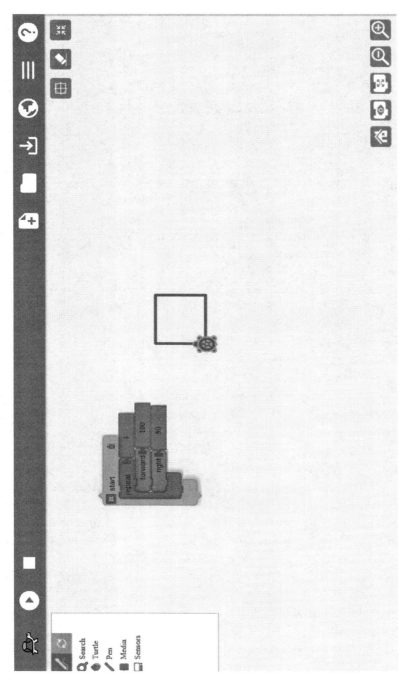

Figure 3.1 A program in Turtle Blocks to draw a square.

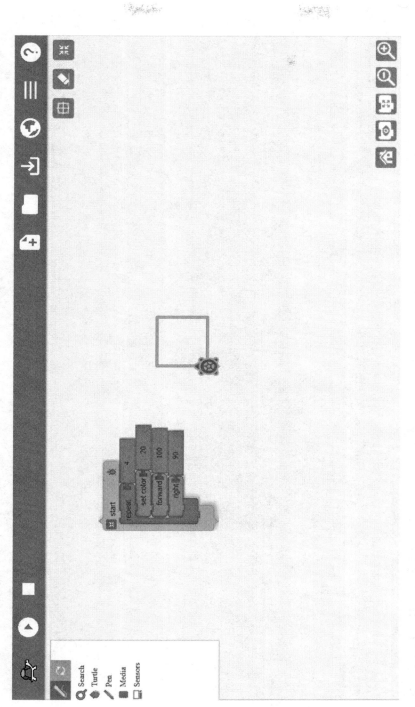

Figure 3.2 A program in Turtle Blocks to draw a square with a specific color on each side.

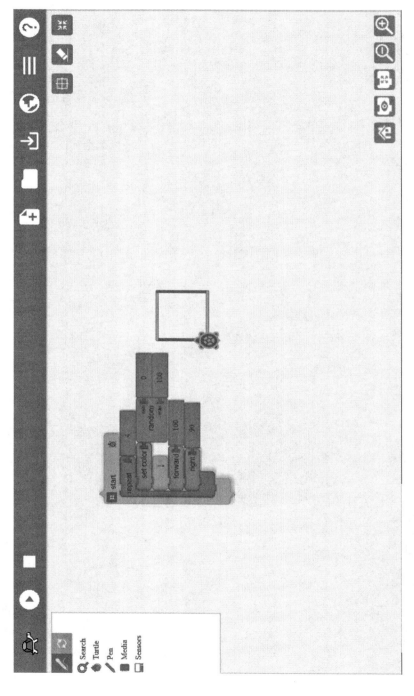

Figure 3.3 A program in Turtle Blocks that draws a square with a randomly generated color on each side.

If they want to make any changes, they would have to change it in each iteration of the code. Through a series of exercises intended to stretch students' comfort with abstraction, they arrive at a point where they can think about how to efficiently program. Not just make it work, but work well. In CS lingo, we talk about using functions to achieve this, or what Turtle Blocks calls "actions." It is like trying to say something in as few words as possible, without losing the meaning.

In Turtle Blocks, the user creates a function, say, drawing a square with a randomly generated color on each side, and can then use this function over and over again. This is another example where Gerald managed the level of abstraction exposed to students. He found it most useful to introduce actions in Turtle Blocks through this type of challenge: the moment when what students are trying to do builds on what they have done before but requires a conceptual leap. That is the ideal time to have them experience new functionality. Figure 3.4 depicts a program in Turtle Blocks that makes use of actions to create reusable functions, and Figure 3.5 depicts this action being used by multiple turtles simultaneously.

Next, Gerald worked to have students understand and apply the notion of variables. Variables allow for adding complexity to a program by allowing that program to respond to changes in inputs. This can be a very difficult concept for young students to grasp, so Gerald located it within the next challenge. He asked students to create a numerical counter, just like they have seen in video games of various types. A typical solution to this challenge involves creating a box in Turtle Blocks, naming that box, assigning it an initial value, and then incrementing that value as the program proceeds (see Figure 3.6.).

In this program, the student reused the function she created earlier to draw a square with a randomly generated color on each side. She wanted her program to draw a circle of squares, which she accomplished by having her turtle "call" that action, then turn two degrees to the right. This set of instructions repeated 10,000 times, resulting in a circle of squares. The counter allowed her to see the number of squares her program drew. The "print" block displayed the value of the counter variable on the screen.

The last skill students needed in order to successfully complete phase 1 of the project was "sensing." Sensing allows the program to use information from the outside world or within the world of the program to change the function of the program itself. For example, students often encounter video games that keep track of a character's health. When their character's health falls below a certain level (the condition), the character dies. Gerald challenged his class to add both sensing and conditional statements to result in changes to their program, adding both variables and complexity.

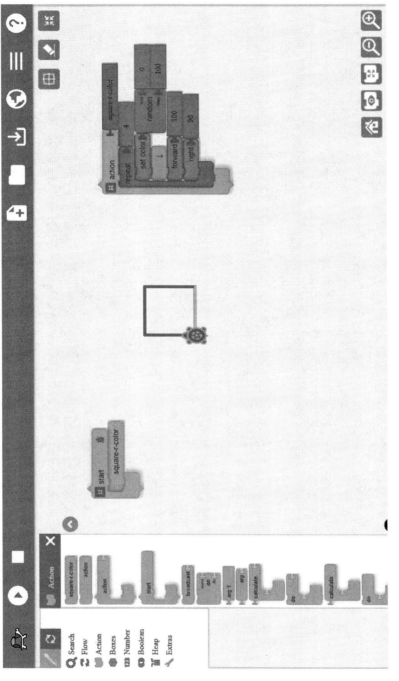

Figure 3.4 A program in Turtle Blocks using the "action" functionality.

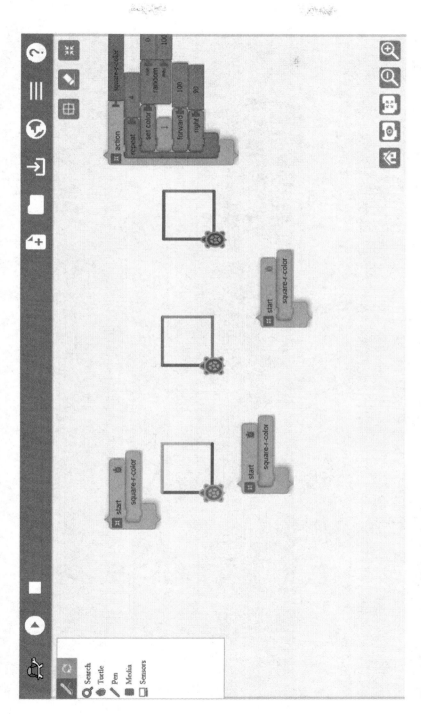

Figure 3.5 A program in Turtle Blocks applying an "action" to multiple turtles simultaneously.

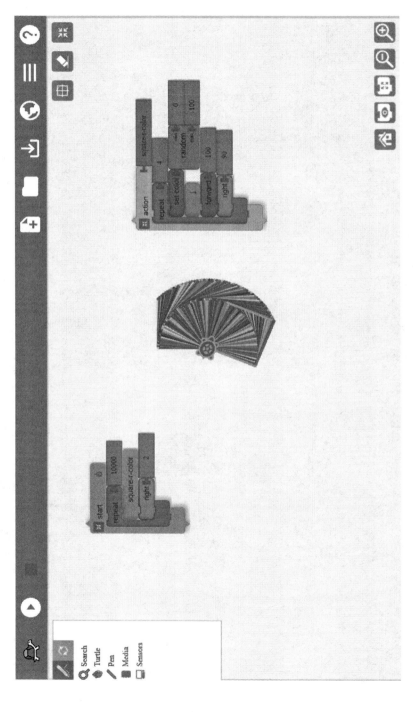

Figure 3.6 A program in Turtle Blocks using a box (variable) to count the number of squares generated.

They didn't disappoint.

One possible solution to this challenge was to have the program in Turtle Blocks monitor the sound level (via the computer's microphone) and then to take a set of actions based on this input. In this program, after the turtle has drawn one hundred squares (which is monitored by the counter variable), it stops and says, "I need a nap!" It's an interactive device programmed in Turtle Block (see Figure 3.7.).

This phase of the project, *Block-Based Coding with Turtle Blocks,* provided Gerald's students with a set of challenges during which they mastered core CS skills: creating instructions, functions, variables, and conditional statements. And just as importantly, students did so in a student-centered, inquiry-based learning environment that allowed them to explore Turtle Blocks at their own pace and create programs that were meaningful to them. Gerald worked with individual students to manage abstraction so that they could make the appropriate cognitive leaps at exactly the point at which they were ready for them.

Then, Gerald ushered the class into the project's second phase.

Phase 2: Text-Based Coding in Python

In the next phase of his project, *Designing and Coding an Interactive Device in Python Turtle,* Gerald introduced his seventh graders to text-based coding in Python. He selected Python because 1) it's free and runs on every operating system, 2) the code is reader friendly, and 3) there are lots of online resources available to support the learner. In particular, Gerald used the Python Turtle library, which contains all the bits necessary to create programs that draw shapes just like Turtle Blocks.

So, as with Turtle Blocks, students were shown how to create a turtle and to have the turtle draw a square (see Figure 3.8.). However, unlike Turtle Blocks, where the turtles themselves and their instructions already exist as blocks, Gerald began to have students understand that these things must be done explicitly in Python.

Let's look at what is actually happening in this program in terms of what the Python code says and the result (see Table 3.1.).

Gerald found that at this point many students realize they want to know what is actually happening with the code. For example, they ask, "Can you use anything for the color?" Gerald encourages, 'Give it a try and see what happens.' Students soon find out that Python recognizes only some colors through words,

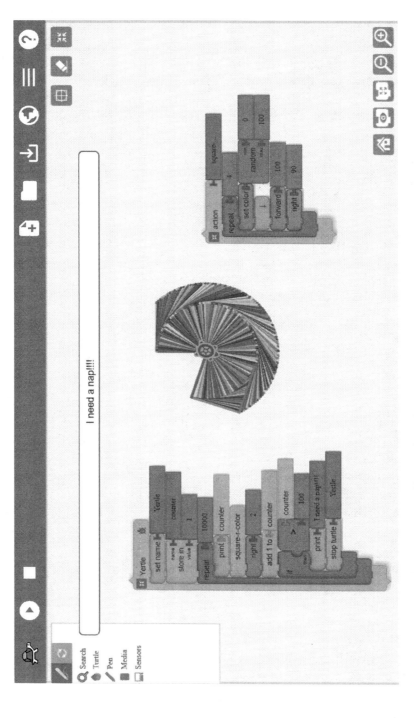

Figure 3.7 A Turtle Blocks program that adds a conditional statement.

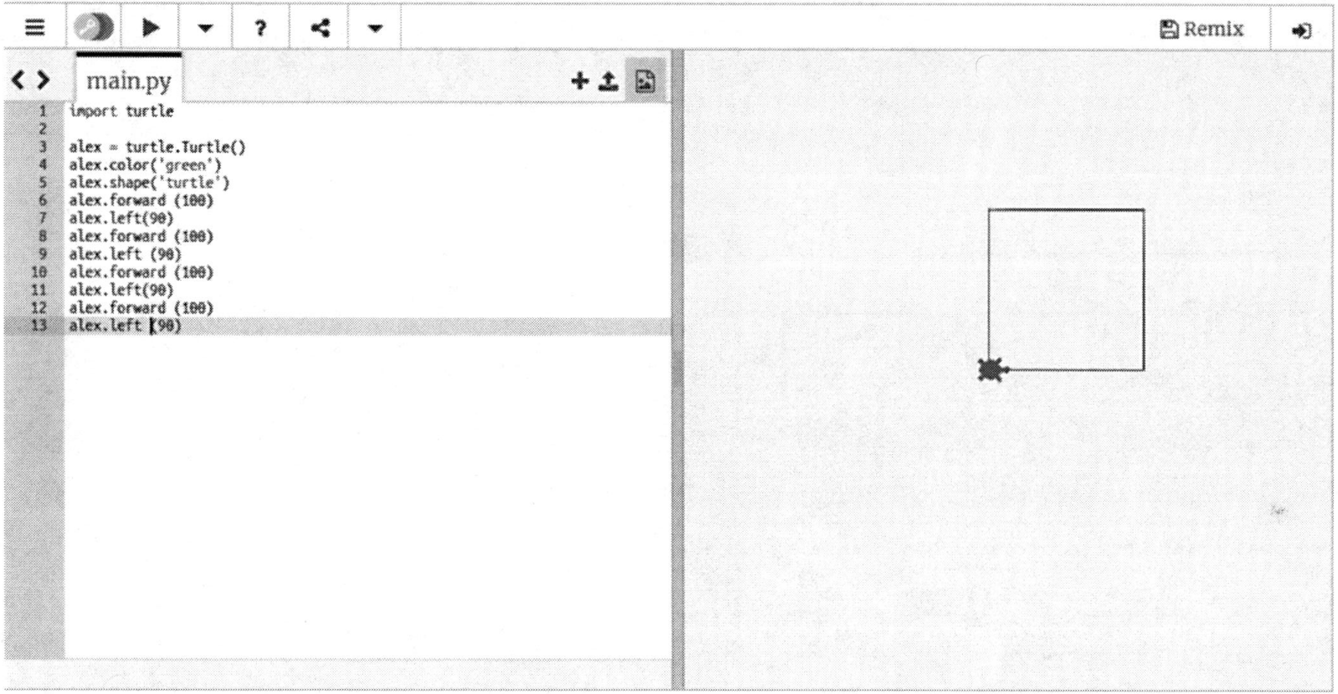
Remix
main.py
1 import turtle
2
3 alex = turtle.Turtle()
4 alex.color('green')
5 alex.shape('turtle')
6 alex.forward (100)
7 alex.left(90)
8 alex.forward (100)
9 alex.left (90)
10 alex.forward (100)
11 alex.left(90)
12 alex.forward (100)
13 alex.left (90)

Figure 3.8 A program in Python Turtle to draw a square.

Abstraction

Table 3.1 A Table Breaking Down Python Turtle Code and What It Does

Python Turtle Code	What Is Actually Happening
Import Turtle	Go get the Python Turtle library with all of its functionality.
alex = turtle.turtle()	Go to the Python Turtle library, find the object called "Turtle," and bring one to my program.
alex.color ('green')	Assign the color green to my turtle called alex.
alex.shape ('turtle')	Assign the shape turtle to my turtle called alex.
alex.forward (100)	Move my turtle called alex 100 pixels in the direction he is pointed.
alex.left (90)	Move my turtle called alex 90 degrees to the right.

which gets them ready for the next challenge, which is about having each side of their square first having a predetermined different color and then, ultimately, a randomly generated color. To do this, they have to develop another abstraction—how does the Python language define color?

Students worked through the sequence of coding challenges as they had in Turtle Blocks. First, they created a square that had a different color on each side (see Figure 3.9). To meet this challenge, the students did not have to learn any new skills. Rather, they applied the color method three more times, once to each remaining side of their squares.

Next, students were introduced to the "repeat" functionality in Python, which makes use of the "for loop" (see Figure 3.10). Again, let's walk through this line by line (see Table 3.2).

The next challenge, as before with Turtle Blocks, was for students to create a program that defined a function square (analogous to the action functionality in Turtle Blocks). Figure 3.11 depicts this program.

Gerald introduced this functionality in terms of Turtle Blocks ("This is how you create actions in Python Turtle") so that his students could make the necessary connection. They came to see that the code was something they had seen before.

Remember *def square ( ): ?*

It worked the same way they saw the "action" block work in Turtle Blocks. Gerald joked that it is far more cumbersome to explain this to adults than it is to middle school children. Also as before, he provided a model, which they then copied and played with. The students then explored ways to define other functions, like those that drew rectangles or triangles.

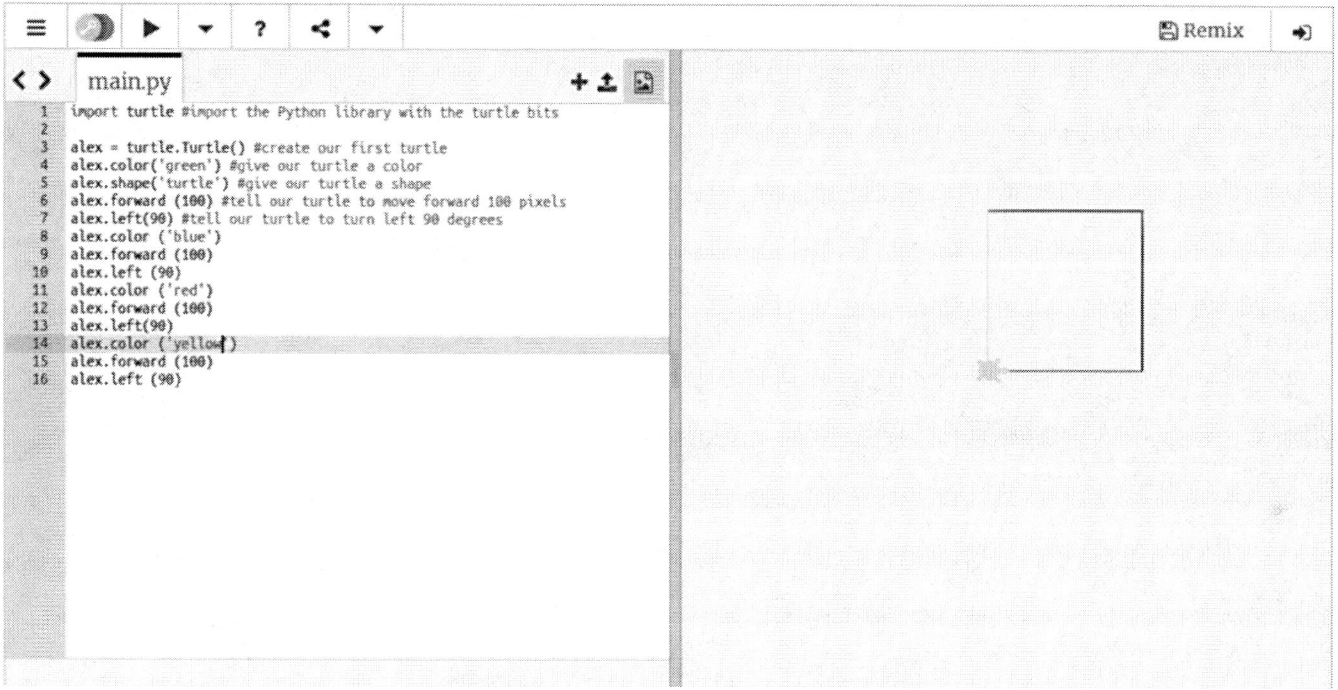

```
import turtle #import the Python library with the turtle bits

alex = turtle.Turtle() #create our first turtle
alex.color('green') #give our turtle a color
alex.shape('turtle') #give our turtle a shape
alex.forward(100) #tell our turtle to move forward 100 pixels
alex.left(90) #tell our turtle to turn left 90 degrees
alex.color ('blue')
alex.forward (100)
alex.left (90)
alex.color ('red')
alex.forward (100)
alex.left(90)
alex.color ('yellow')
alex.forward (100)
alex.left (90)
```

Figure 3.9 A program in Python Turtle to draw a square with a different color for each side.

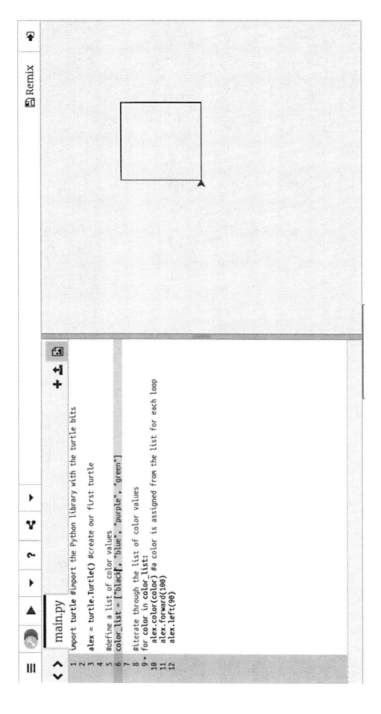

Figure 3.10 A program in Python Turtle to draw a square with a different color for each side using a for loop.

Table 3.2 A Table Showing Color Alteration in Python Turtle

Python Turtle Code	What Is Actually Happening
Import Turtle	Go get the Python Turtle library with all of its functionality.
alex = turtle.turtle()	Go to the Python Turtle library, find the object called "Turtle," and bring one to my program.
alex.color ('green')	Assign the color green to my turtle called alex.
alex.shape ('turtle')	Assign the shape turtle to my turtle called alex.
alex.forward (100)	Move my turtle called alex 100 pixels in the direction he is pointed.
alex.left (90)	Move my turtle called alex 90 degrees to the right.
alex.color ('blue')	Assign the color blue to my turtle called alex.
alex.forward (100)	Move my turtle called alex 100 pixels in the direction he is pointed.
alex.left (90)	Move my turtle called alex 90 degrees to the right.
alex.color ('red')	Assign the color red to my turtle called alex.
alex.forward (100)	Move my turtle called alex 100 pixels in the direction he is pointed.
alex.left (90)	Move my turtle called alex 90 degrees to the right.
alex.color ('yellow')	Assign the color yellow to my turtle called alex.
alex.forward (100)	Move my turtle called alex 100 pixels in the direction he is pointed.
alex.left (90)	Move my turtle called alex 90 degrees to the right.

The last challenge involved having the students draw squares that had a randomly generated color on each side, as they had in Turtle Blocks. This challenge required the highest level of abstraction. As they had seen before, the Python language understands colors as numbers. However, Python defines colors using the RGB (red, green, blue) system, which specifies each color as mixes of those three primary colors. In this system, each color as represented as a triplet of numbers between 0 and 255. For example, purple is represented as (155, 21, 255), meaning it has some red (155), very little green (21), and lots of blue (255). In Gerald's experience, students love learning this.

The next abstraction is about how Python operationalizes randomness. As we saw earlier, the students came to understand how Turtle Blocks dealt with randomness via a Random block, as depicted in Figure 3.9. So, now students had to learn how Python deals with randomness and that the Random block in Turtle Blocks picks a new number within a user-defined range each time the program uses it. In Python, they first need to understand that this functionality also lives

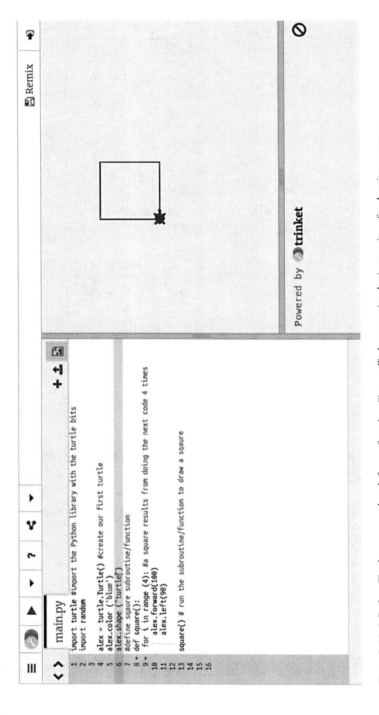

Figure 3.11 A Python Turtle program that defines a function ("square") that contains the instructions for drawing a square.

in a library called *random,* which has a method called random.randint (which means "from the *random* library, grab the function *randint,* which picks a random integer"). So, their code needs to include it as well as the Turtle library. Then they just need to see an example of how this is done. Gerald gives them the code snippet random.randit (0, 255). He encouraged them to treat it just like a block they have to include in their Python program. This code snippet generates a random number in the range indicated in the parentheses. In order to generate a random color, we would need a set of three random numbers, each of which is between 0 and 255 (see Figure 3.12.).

By the end of these challenges, Gerald's seventh-grade students had by and large successfully navigated the transition from block-based to text-based coding. They were certainly not expert programmers, nor was that Gerald's goal. His goal was to provide a learning environment in which they would be able to code by typing words. And it worked. They were writing usable code in Python.

Phase 3: Text-Based Coding in Arduino

By the end of the Python Turtle work, Gerald felt his students were ready to tackle the next level of complexity and abstraction, namely, building and coding interactive devices using the Arduino microprocessor and its associated software IDE. That's a whole lot of polysyllabic babble. Let's break it down.

The Arduino microprocessor board is an inexpensive (about $30) miniature computer that can be used as the core (the brain) of interactive devices. Figure 3.13 depicts a device built with the Arduino. This device is a circuit that includes a red light called a light-emitting diode (LED).

The circuit is a simple one. The LED is controlled by pin 13 on the Arduino board, and its wiring utilizes a resistor that protects the LED from burning out. The simple circuit returns to the Arduino via the GROUND pin. It's that easy. The circuit comes to life, so to speak, through some coding that results in the LED blinking on and off. Allow me to explain what the code you see in Figure 3.14 actually says. We'll do it one step at a time.

This program has the same two main components of any Arduino program: *setup* and *loop.* The *setup* portion of the program literally sets up what's needed for the program to work: pinMode(LED_BUILTIN, OUTPUT). In this case, the piece of code declares that our program will talk to the built-in LED (which happens to be on pin 13). The *loop* portion of the code details the instructions, which will repeat over and over again (looping) as long as the Arduino board has

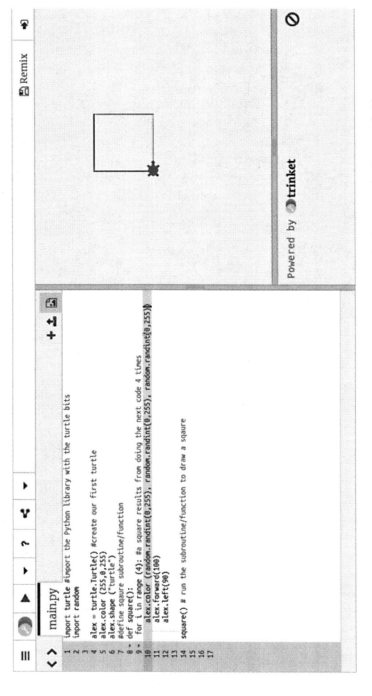

Figure 3.12 A Python Turtle program that defines a function that draws a square with a randomly generated color on each side.

Abstraction

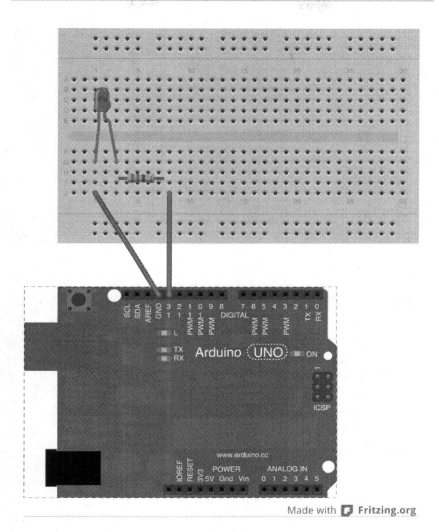

Figure 3.13 Arduino device for blinking an LED.

power. In this case the LED pin is set to HIGH (which means "on") for 1 second (1,000 milliseconds):

```
digitalWrite(LED_BUILTIN, HIGH);
delay(1000);
```

and then set to LOW (which means "off") for another second (1,000 milliseconds):

```
digitalWrite(LED_BUILTIN, LOW);
delay(1000);
```

Abstraction

Figure 3.14 Simple program in Arduino for blinking an LED.

Clearly, even this chunk of code requires that students understand different levels of abstraction. HIGH and LOW stand in for turning the LED on and off. Seconds are understood by the Arduino program in terms of milliseconds. Special words (like *delay*) and punctuation (like semicolons) give the program its intended meaning. In Arduino, as with other text-based coding languages, the syntax is less visually scaffolded and intuitive. It must be explicitly taught and learned.

Once students understood this pattern (and this abstraction) about how sensors, variables, and conditional statements work, they were able to apply it to other sensors and other behaviors. For example, a pair of students built a circuit that utilized an ultrasound sensor. An ultrasound sensor works like echolocation in bats and other organisms. One part of the sensor emits an ultrasound pulse and then receives that pulse when it is bounced off an object. The delay between these two events can be used to determine distance. Students used the data received from this sensor to control the speed and direction (backwards or forwards) of a motor. This is the beginning of an obstacle avoidance program for a robot—like those automated vacuum cleaners you see nowadays.

Phase 4: Exhibit and Reflect

Gerald's students reported finding phase 3 of the project the most difficult. This is certainly understandable. The Arduino code is far less intuitive than either the block-based code in Turtle Blocks or the human-friendly code in Python Turtle. The students loved the physicality of the circuits themselves. However, the physicality of needing to build circuits—along with understanding the fundamentals of wires, LEDs, resistors, and photocells—added to the complexity and the resulting levels of abstraction. Nonetheless, by the end of this part of his feedback mechanism project, just about all of Gerald's students had successfully designed and coded interactive devices that utilized the Arduino microprocessor.

On the surface, this work seems quite credibly to be about CS and CT skills. But it is far more about using these skills to deepen students' understanding of science, specifically. Certainly, the students were very engaged and challenged by creating an interactive device through text-based coding. They worked hard and generally met and overcame challenges. They learned to debug code successfully for the most part. In these ways, in Gerald's experience, this type of program seems to support the development of self-regulatory skills.

And yet there is something about supporting students in navigating the various levels of abstraction that Gerald believes is the most rewarding component of this work. The first time, for example, that students uncover that the code they are working with reads colors as a set of numbers within a specific range (as with the RGB code related earlier) or they see that sensors (like those in their cell phones) merely take data from the outside world and convert it to changes in the flow of electricity and that this information can be used to control other behaviors, their minds are blown in ways that are unique and powerful and cool—all at the same time.

 ## Uncovering Subconcepts

This chapter has focused on the key concept of abstraction and its subconcepts decomposition, pattern recognition, generalization and detail removal, modularity, and interfaces. Each of these has been illustrated in the description of Gerald's interactive machine project with his seventh-grade science students. Throughout the project, Gerald orchestrated students' experiences with abstraction and its subconcepts. Additionally, he orchestrated the management of levels of abstraction as a matter of pedagogy and created a productive learning environment for these novice programmers. Let's take a look.

Decomposition

According to the Blueprint, **decomposition** is defined as "ideas, problems, or projects [. . .] broken down into component parts to set the stage for deeper analysis." In Gerald's project, we can see decomposition as a key element that he included in each of the challenges described. Perhaps the most salient example revolves around students learning that Turtle Blocks and Python's Turtle library both decompose colors into numbers. In the case of Turtle Blocks, these numbers take the form of values between 0 and 100, and colors have properties such as hue and chroma (which Gerald did not cover with his students). As we saw in Python, colors are defined as triplets of numbers, which correspond to the RGB system. In both cases, in order to effectively deal with colors in their programs, students had to learn to decompose their intuitive and descriptive experience of colors into ones that involve abstraction and decomposition—and numbers.

Pattern Recognition

According to the Blueprint, **pattern recognition** is defined as "decomposed component parts [. . .] examined to find patterns like similarities, repetition, conditional relationships, or nested relationships." One of the turning points in Gerald's programming project with his seventh-grade science students took place during their initial exposure to the Arduino language, which was by far the most abstract of the three programming languages. To introduce them to the language, Gerald had projected onto a smartboard the Arduino code for a program that blinked an LED on and off (see again Figure 3.14).

Gerald began by asking students to try to figure out what the code was doing. They could readily determine that HIGH and LOW was the same as on and off and that the delay was pretty much what it seemed to be. The real conceptual leap happened when some students made the connection between the **setup** and **loop** elements as being the same as blocks. Once they did, students suddenly began to find Arduino more like something they already knew than something completely new to them. Gerald worked to leverage these types of experiences throughout this project.

Generalization and Detail Removal

According to the Blueprint, **generalization and detail removal** is defined as "component parts [...] grouped by general characteristics, and unnecessary details [are] filtered out." From the very beginning of the feedback mechanism project, Gerald worked to have his students first do something and then step back and generalize what they had done. For example, when his students began to work in Turtle Blocks, the first challenge Gerald gave them was to write a program that would draw a square. For many of them, this involved four sets of instructions: move forward, turn right; move forward, turn right; move forward, turn right; move forward, turn right. Once they had done this successfully, Gerald asked them to try to do the same thing with the fewest number of instructions (revisit Figure 3.4). This step had them see that only two things were happening (moving forward and turning right) and that these things could then be repeated as needed. Gerald repeated this type of pattern of challenge and then generalization/detail removal through his work with each of the three programming languages.

Modularity

According to the NYC DOE Blueprint, **modularity** is defined as "a process that completes a single task [that] is more useful when it can be chained together with other processes to accomplish something more complex." During the project, Gerald highlighted this subconcept in each of the three programming languages. In Turtle Blocks, for example, modularity was accomplished via the Action blocks (see Figure 3.4). In Python, modularity was accomplished through the use of functions (see Figure 3.12). In Arduino, the structure of its programs includes two modular components, namely **setup** and **loop** (see Figure 3.14). Gerald continued to have his students understand that programming became efficient when sections of code could be made modular and that these modules could be reused both within and across programs. In fact, Gerald came to feel that modularity could be used to assess students' understanding of programming concepts.

Abstraction

Interfaces

In this project, Gerald's students had to learn to interact effectively with several **interfaces**: one for Turtle Blocks, which included simple features like compatible shapes indicating compatible functionality; one for Python, which, being text based, included potential errors stemming from typos; and one for Arduino, which introduced the increased requirements of its programming language. According to the NYC DOE Blueprint, "Interfaces help users complete tasks, while hiding details of the overall process."

Gerald discovered that the way each interface handled the processing of programming errors ultimately became its most salient feature. Students had to learn to recognize, interpret, and address these various interface-specific error messages. For example, Turtle Blocks generates a warning sign with arrows directing the programmer to the area of concern. Python highlights the line of code and provides some description of the error. The Arduino IDE will also highlight the line of code and provide some description. Typically, students felt Arduino error messages to be the most abstract.

In Gerald's experience, a key part of students' success in learning to program is developing a capacity for recognizing, interpreting, and responding to these various types of error messages. This became the key activity in Gerald's classroom once the students became familiar with the coding basics in each language. He also found that encouraging students to share their experiences with one another in a peer mentoring model became a very effective strategy to help students be able to deal powerfully with this interface-based feedback.

In Sum

This chapter has focused on the CS concept of abstraction and its subconcepts of pattern recognition, generalization/detail removal, modularity, and interfaces. In addition, this chapter explored a connection to pedagogical strategies used by all successful teachers to orchestrate the levels of abstraction within a content area or skill in ways that allow students to engage powerful with in and thereby lead to mastery. A key component of this work for Gerald was the pedagogical strategy of orchestrating and managing levels of abstraction for and with his students in ways that allowed them to be able to respond to increasing levels of complexity and challenges effectively and powerfully.

The pedagogical moves described here themselves fall into a pattern. First, regardless of the coding language used (Scratch, Turtle Blocks, Python, or Arduino) teach some basic CS skills. For example, in Turtle Blocks, the basic skills include that one programs by snapping blocks together, as well as key blocks, like forward, right, etc. Then, design challenges that allow students to apply these skills in ways that are meaningful to them. Again, in Turtle Blocks, the students were challenged to create a program that produced a square with each side having a randomly generated color. These challenges should be orchestrated to anticipate and lead students to the functionality (like Actions in Turtle Blocks, RGB color syntax, and setting pins in Arduino) that are essential but almost impossible to discover. Once students are engaged in these challenges, it then becomes possible to introduce them to this high level of abstraction, usually in a one-to-one or small group setting. By this point, to paraphrase the great math educator Dan Myer, students have a headache and the abstraction becomes the aspirin.

We discussed these various types of abstraction through the description of a project that Gerald designed and conducted with his seventh-grade science students. His project focused on the science concept of feedback mechanisms and allowed students to design and model feedback mechanisms using tools that support computationality. The project gave students experience with block-based programming in Turtle Blocks, an introduction to text-based coding using Python's Turtle functionality, and, finally, the opportunity to build circuits and create programs that control them in Arduino.

Connections to Content Areas

The recognition and development of abstraction are fundamental to any deep learning on the part of students in any discipline. Good teachers skillfully orchestrate abstraction with their content areas, as well as levels of abstraction in the introduction of new concepts, skills, and content. Let's take a look at what this could look like in these content areas.

English Language Arts

Reading and writing are all about abstraction. Young children learn that letters of the alphabet represent sounds, that words are representations of collections of sounds. Reading is all about decomposition and pattern recognition. When children are reading, we already ask them to identify things like character traits, or setting, or a narrative flow. In our normal teaching of these things, we could easily make transparent the concept of abstraction (and its subconcepts of pattern recognition and modularity). Gerald worked with a teacher who designed a project with her high school students where they made a graph of the evolution of characters in *The Lord of the Flies*. In her project, the students saw immediately the evolution of these characters across the book.

History

The study of history is very much about the discovery and application of trends over time. Abstraction, then, is fundamental to the study and practice of history. Students can be taught to ask the kinds of questions that allow them to uncover and apply these trends. Under which conditions does oppression generate revolution? What factors are associated with the rise and fall of governments? Why are some people richer or more powerful than others? All of these questions are typical in the teaching and learning of history, and each allows students to interact powerfully with the practice of abstraction.

Science

This chapter focused on some ways to engage student inquiry in science through the use of abstraction. Scientific inquiry across the grade levels is all about discovering patterns. What happens when hot and cold things come together? What happens when two objects collide? How does electricity work? Certainly tools that support computationality as we have seen in this chapter can be applied across grade levels. Systems of all types can be modeled as diagrams, in three dimensions, and through software.

Math

When children and adults say, as they too often do, that they hate math, they tend to ask the same question: "When am I ever going to use [insert math skill here] in real life?" Underlying this question is an inherent suggestion that abstractions are central to math, but not life. How untrue! In our normal teaching of math, we already teach students different levels of abstraction. Numbers can be represented by symbols, and these symbols can be used to represent mathematical thinking.

In addition, the mathematical skills regularly involve pattern recognition ("look, these are all even numbers") and generalization ("any number multiplied by 1 is itself), and modularity (3 + 2 is the same as 2 + 3). Programming tools can be broadly used for math instruction. For example, students can create function machines at pretty much any age level, bringing math and life together right before their eyes.

The Arts

When Gerald taught middle school, his art colleague had designed a project in which students created tessellations with sixth-grade students. You know: those M. C. Escher drawings where staircases ascend and descend into each other, where shapes and shadows twist and turn in unexpected ways. Central to this project was an understanding of modularity. How do young artists take a particular shape or concept and copy it to repeat, yes, but in new ways? Art teachers teach abstraction when they focus on the common patterns and techniques of different elements of art, such as brushstrokes, color schemes, and composition.

 ## **For Further Exploration**

- Play with | Turtle Blocks: https://turtle.sugarlabs.org/
- Explore | Python Turtle: http://pythonturtle.org/
- Read | An introduction to Arduino: https://create.arduino.cc/projecthub/projects/tags/kids

Algorithms

You would think that someone who bought a multihundred-dollar chessboard was actually good at chess. Such is not the case. Tom is terrible at chess, a rudimentary player whose complete lack of a coherent strategy becomes obvious after the first few moves. But he loves playing it. And there was something special about this particular chess set that was simply irresistible.

On this chessboard, your opponent's pieces move themselves. No joke. The chessboard is designed so one person can play on their physical board without their opponent nearby. Your opponent can be on the other side of the world, playing you on a special mobile app. When they move pieces on their mobile phone, the pieces on Tom's chessboard in New York City move on their own.

Algorithms abound in this example. The Blueprint team defines algorithms as "a generalized and repeatable sequence of instructions that achieve a particular purpose and output, given a set of inputs." Let's unpack further what algorithms are.

The game of chess itself is inherently algorithmic. Each piece on the board has limited kinds of moves it can make. For instance, a pawn can only move one space forward at a time, except on the first move, when it can move two, or if it is taking another piece, which it can only do diagonally. Each of the clauses in that previous sentence comprises "a generalized and repeatable sequence of instruction that achieve[s] a particular purpose." The "purpose" is to play chess. Every kind of piece on the board has a comparable algorithmic logic. When you start to play a game of chess, you have to weigh which moves are most beneficial in both the short and long term. Your mind operates computationally: "If I move my pawn there, then I can force my opponent to move her knight out of position. That might help weaken her defense later." What you begin to see is that not only are repeatable instructions algorithmic but so is planning for multiple possibilities. You can begin to branch out in a choose-your-own-adventure way of thinking.

People think algorithmically all the time. Have you ever watched someone's face when they are running late for a connection at an airport, when a subway line is down, or when there is traffic on their usual route home? If you could listen to their thought process, it would reveal a series of possible ways they envision getting to where they need to go—all weighing the limitations and possibilities of each route and all with alternatives in mind should some options prove untenable.

We might refer to what we just explored as analogue algorithms. That is, there are no digital computers involved. However, the very same logic undergirds the digital world.

Tom's wine-induced enthusiasm noted earlier for the chessboard did not appear out of nowhere. He had seen a YouTube video advertising it the previous week, but thought it too expensive. Come Thanksgiving, while scrolling through Instagram, ads for the chessboard began appearing in his feed over and over. Tom was tightly targeted for those advertisements in a digital world where social media companies share user data to deliver just-in-time marketing primed for specific people to act on in a specific moment. The digital marketing world thrives on sophisticated algorithmic logic. Tom has the chessboard to prove it.

Rock, Paper, Scissors Battles

When the eyes of 200 elementary and middle school students fix on you, the noise briefly calmed, you have about 7.4 seconds to earn their continued attention. That window of time is not at all scientific, no empirical study to justify its statement. Just gut instinct. Tom got right to it. "Welcome to our camp on computational thinking!" Not really an attention grabber. Too many syllables. He went on.

"We are about to hold a first-of-its-kind tournament where only one of you here today will be named champion!"

That was more like it.

"How many of you have ever played Rock, Paper, Scissors?" Hands shot up throughout the cafeteria in which they gathered. He went on.

"Excellent. Here's how it will go. Each of you is sitting at a table with your team of about twenty students and several teachers. Your teachers will help facilitate a practice round in which everyone plays a three-round match. The victors of those practice rounds will go to the right side of the room. The nonvictors will go to the left side of the room. You have three minutes. Go!"

With that, children turned to each other with a range of expressions on their faces. Some seemed dazed, overwhelmed by the sheer number of other human

Algorithms

beings in close proximity whose volume levels abruptly rose and whose arms began swinging and darting through the air. Others wore visages of concentrated competition. They chanted—rock, paper, scissors, shoot—and quickly dispensed with their opponents. As the battles were won and lost, teachers ushered the students to the two sides of the room.

"Now, we have two teams. Over the next few minutes, your teams will conduct a best-of-three series of Rock, Paper, Scissor battles. If you lose, just step toward the outside near the wall and cheer on others. Your team has to determine one representative who will compete against the other side of the room for the championship. Keep battling it out within your team until there is one student remaining, then send them up to the front of the room. Please begin."

And so the rounds continued, the giddy hollers of "rock, paper, scissors, shoot" echoing all around. Little by little, the crowds on both sides began to give way to clusters of smaller challenges. Ultimately, each side sent up their finalists to the small stage at the front of the room.

The two students, a boy and a girl, introduced themselves to the yelps of their respective teams. They shook hands like prize fighters and began. After three expert rounds, the girl raised her hands in victory. Tom proudly presented her with the coveted "air trophy," which, as the title suggests, was a giant nonexistent award composed of air. (Despite its fairly clear title, the student was nevertheless visibly disappointed.) As the finalists returned to their teams amidst a buzz of congratulatory remarks, Tom congratulated the entire room on what he considered the most important victory to be: "You have all just demonstrated beyond a shadow of a doubt that you know far more about computationality than you might imagine."

For many months leading up to it, Tom worked with his colleague Hannah Gerber to design a two-week professional learning experience for pre-service teachers as part of a grant in computational thinking. As briefly described in Chapter 2, the first week focused on teaching teachers about computationality through a series of learning experiences. The second week put teachers in charge of groups of students, whom they guided through similar learning experiences. As in this book, Tom and Hannah wanted to make sure that they inverted the usual way teachers learned about computationality. Whereas many approaches focus on applying computational principles and practices to classroom instruction from the outside or plugging computer science exercises into one's lesson, they wanted to tease out ways that computationality already operated in participants' lives, both inside and outside school. Instead of putting teachers through traditional professional development workshops, they designed the first week of the camp to be more like a "computational carnival," with a series of loosely connected kinds of activities that together created a patchwork of computational learning: smart, fun, and hands-on.

One of the core challenges was to resist their instincts on how to design computational learning experiences. It was easy to imagine giving students access to web-based coding platforms that offered engaging introductory exercises in programming. But that wasn't quite what Tom and Hannah were after. Computationality was already a part of everyone's lives. If they could craft ways for teachers and students to uncover what they already know about computationality, they theorized that learners would feel more empowered to continue exploring computer science afterward. When they began discussing ways to introduce algorithms to teachers, Tom and Hannah quickly found themselves considering the usual YouTube videos in which mathematicians and computer scientists explain how algorithms are formulated and what function they serve in software. The problem with relying solely and too early on videos is that it perpetuates the idea that learning is a matter of learners absorbing information. That's nearly never true. As Tom often repeated during those two weeks: Learning isn't about teachers covering content; it is about students uncovering understanding. What were ways to help teachers and students uncover what they already knew about algorithms?

As the noise in the room settled, Tom repeated the idea to the group that they already knew way more about computationality than they realized. And not just computationality. But algorithms.

"Let us prove it to you. In your teams, take the next few minutes to discuss something with your teammates. For every round of Rock, Paper, Scissors you played, how did you determine whether to throw rock or paper or scissors? Everyone has their own strategy. What was yours? Your teachers will help facilitate and prepare to share some of your insights with the whole group. Your time starts now."

Stopwatch in hand, Tom circulated to listen in on how students approached the game. In the distance, he saw a small group of boys animatedly demonstrating to each other different ways they had decided to throw their hands. It was hard to hone in on individual sentences from any one group as the collective chatter in the room crunched along inaudibly. After three minutes, Tom called everyone back to share.

"Who'd like to start?"

59

"We will," asserted one of the teachers as she took the microphone. She invited up one of the students, an eleven-year-old who appeared to have given the matter a great deal of thought.

"I always start with rock. But I don't really expect to win the first round. I just want to see what they throw. Whatever they throw, I will throw next time whatever beats them. So if they throw scissors the first round I will throw rock in the second round. But if they throw paper I will throw scissors."

Whispers unfurled in the room like a blanket being placed on the ground for a picnic.

Then another team raised their hand. They took the mic. A nine-year-old student shared his strategy.

"I just go random. I don't want my opponent to have any idea what I am going to throw. If I am random, then they can't ever figure out what I'm going to do. But they will keep trying to figure it out and get frustrated. That gives me an advantage."

This idea was greeted with a swell of discussion in the room. Some participants shook their heads in disagreement that a randomized Rock, Paper, Scissors approach would work. Others seemed to view it as the most brilliant battle strategy since Hannibal crossed the Alps to romp through Italy.

In planning the week's activities, one of the most important concepts for participants to uncover was the idea that algorithms are intentional and instructive. You will often hear them described as recipes or dance moves. (In fact, Hannah conducted a fantastic activity that guided participants in piecing together the steps in the Macarena, followed by decomposing the steps in the Floss. If you want to see a room full of middle schoolers get fired up, ask them to document the precise steps necessary to perform the Floss. Madness will ensue.)

Now that teachers had uncovered questions and insights about the nature of algorithms, Tom and Hannah showed a clip from a BBC documentary by Oxford professor of mathematics Marcus du Sautoy to illustrate the instructive nature of algorithms. In the video, du Sautoy sets up a little experiment on the famed campus. On a small table over which is draped a red and white checkered tablecloth, he sets a large glass jar. In the jar, he places thirteen chocolates wrapped in gold foil—and one red hot chili pepper. The affable professor then invites unsuspecting students to play a little game with him. They will each take a turn retrieving candies from the jar in amounts of one to three at a time. Whoever is left with the chili, well, you know what happens.

It seems like a simple game in which both participants have a fair chance to win. After all, you can select one or two or three candies at a time. As long as you are thinking ahead, you should be able to force your opponent to wind up running for a glass of milk (or tequila, maybe). But du Sautoy always wins. He wins because he has a trick up his sleeve. As he later reveals, "Whatever my opponent does, my algorithm tells me how to respond." He always chooses first; he always chooses one chocolate to start. And with that, his opponent is already doomed. Here's why, in his own words:

"So, the key is to think about grouping things in fours. Thirteen chocolates divides into three groups of four, with one left over. So, by taking one chocolate in the first round, and then four minus whatever the other person takes in the subsequent rounds, this algorithm ensures that the other player is always left with the chili."

The clip helps playfully drive home the instructive nature of algorithms—that they are like recipes or dance moves. But it also alludes to the intentionality inherent in algorithms, that someone designed the algorithm and that their intentions might not always be neutral or kind.

Recall the Blueprint definition. It is not just that algorithms provide "a generalized and repeatable sequence of instructions that achieve a particular purpose and output, given a set of inputs," as described in the first part of its definition. But rather, it is the second sentence in the definition that merits equal or greater attention, especially the last clause: "to understand when, why and how to implement an algorithm, and to consider who or what might be affected." The last clause refers to the intentions of those who compose algorithms, to the ways in which their work has intended and unintended consequences in the world. Algorithms are not just math or computer code. They have very real consequences in peoples' lives, not just hot chilis. Algorithms are used to determine what interest rate you get on a mortgage. Algorithms are used in large school districts to place children into kindergarten and to set the cutoff scores for teacher effectiveness ratings. Algorithms are even used by judges in some counties to sentence criminals to jail. We would go out on a limb to say that your average banker or district official or judge would be hard pressed to explain in any detail what algorithms are and how the way they are formulated can actually perpetuate inequity and discrimination. Algorithms merit severe ethical scrutiny, a feat made all the more challenging because they are often invisible to users and guarded tightly by the companies who produce them.

The Hannibalian child now seated, Tom drew everyone's attention to a slide on the screen. It featured a table.

"Check out the screen at the front of the room. You might not ever have heard of Boolean logic, but everything you just did tells me you know quite a bit about it. Boolean logic is a fundamental principle that makes the whole

Algorithms

Table 4.1 The Rules for Rock, Paper Scissors as Boolean Logic

IF Player 1	AND Player 2	THEN Outcome
Rock	Rock	Tie | Redo
Rock	**Paper**	Win | Player 2
Rock	Scissors	Win | Player 1
Paper	Paper	Tie | Redo
Paper	Rock	Win | Player 1
Paper	**Scissors**	Win | Player 2
Scissors	Scissors	Tie | Redo
Scissors	**Rock**	Win | Player 2
Scissors	Paper	Win | Player 1

computational world operate. It literally dictates how electricity flows through computers. Boolean logic uses 'operators' to say, 'Well, if this thing happens AND this other thing happens, then the OUTPUT will be such and such.' The point is that words you already know like AND, OR, and NOT are the heart and soul of how computers engage with the world."

To be honest, this was a point in the two weeks where Tom realized a little too much of his secondary education background was coming through. Some of the older students seemed to follow. Some of the younger students, whose ages were closer to his son's age, looked like they were getting lost. That didn't stop him from continuing, however. After all, he had a table!

"Just look at the table [Table 4.1] to see precisely how Boolean logic informed the algorithms you yourself used to play Rock, Paper, Scissors."

He proudly stepped aside, waving toward the screen.

"Earlier, some of your peers shared how they decide to throw rock, paper, or scissors. Remember? They said things like, 'If I throw rock and my opponent throws paper, next time I will throw scissors.' The way their minds were working, the way they combined all sorts of information and predictions in order to try and achieve a specific outcome . . . that is inherently algorithmic. They are applying Boolean logic to the game so quickly and so naturally, they are hardly aware of their own computationality."

 ## Uncovering Subconcepts

Recipes; dance moves; sinister chocolate and chili games; and Rock, Paper, Scissors. These examples help define the conceptual contours of algorithms. In addition to such broad definitions, there are four subconcepts that can further one's understanding: algorithm design; control flow; inputs, variables, and outputs; and application. Let's uncover briefly what each of these mean.

Algorithm Design

The Blueprint defines **algorithm design** as "instructions [that] should be general, clear, well-formed, complete, and capable of being executed as intended without confusion." In Rock, Paper, Scissors, the rules of the game were so socialized and commonly known that Tom did not harp on reviewing them. Instead, he showed a simple slide that depicted each of the three hand gestures—a fist for rock, a flattened hand for paper, and an inverted peace sign for scissors—with arrows indicating which gesture beats which gesture. The generally understood instructions for playing the game were as follows: 1) choose a partner, 2) each partner throws rock or paper or scissors per round for three rounds, and 3) whoever wins the best of three rounds is the victor. Then, within those battles, participants revealed that they, too, had their own decision-making algorithm designs for how to increase their chances of winning. Many students expressed that they always began with a particular gesture. This allowed them to confidently begin matches and know how to interpret their opponent's throws. When the one student shared that his second throw would be based on what his opponent throws in the first round, he is putting in place a clear and complete instruction that leaves little room for confusion.

The algorithm design in the chocolate and chili game is a bit more sophisticated. In his game, Professor du Sautoy also puts in place a simple set of instructions to ensure his victories. He always takes the first chocolate. He only takes one chocolate on his inaugural selection. Then, on his next turn, the professor always takes four minus whatever his opponent takes. So, if his opponent takes three chocolates, he takes just one. In both cases, it is interesting to note that both the children playing Rock, Paper, Scissors and the Oxford professor try to control the possibilities before them by knowing what they are going to do to start. Controlling possibilities is a key element of algorithms, as the next subconcept also shows.

Control Flow

Remember the child who confidently argued for randomness as his Rock, Paper, Scissors strategy? Despite its appeal, it lacked what we might call a

Algorithms

logical control flow. According to the Blueprint team, **control flow** refers to "the order in which steps of an algorithm are executed; determined by logical constructs such as IF statements, loops and calls to other procedures." With randomness always the rule, it is impossible to systematically and intentionally increase one's odds of winning. There's no real algorithm at play. Contrast that with the idea that a student will throw their second gesture based on your first gesture, or even that they keep track of what you throw in other rounds, and you see how a sophisticated logic can quickly emerge. As described earlier, it is clearest when we think in terms of IF my opponent throws paper, THEN I will throw scissors. But anyone who has ever played multiple rounds of the game while being on daddy duty and not having sufficient activities to engage the child, as his wife had suggested before leaving the two in a sweltering Manhattan apartment for the day (a completely random example, obviously), can tell you that sometimes loops happen. You know what they look like. After a couple coincidental rounds where the two players each throw the same gesture—rock, rock; paper, paper; scissors, scissors—they both start to hedge if or how to break the tie. They get caught in the tie loop, partly wanting to see who breaks it first and partly too afraid to call the other's bluff. One can design algorithmic approaches to problems, but one must also ensure the fidelity of their implementation.

Inputs, Variables, and Outputs

Inputs, variables, and outputs, as defined in the Blueprint, refer to "how data is passed into (inputs), manipulated, used within (variables), and returned from the algorithm (outputs)." In the chocolates and chilies examples, the way these three elements interplay is very clear. After taking one chili to start, the professor collects data based on his opponent's selection. He has in his mind two variables—let's call them x (how many chocolates his opponent chooses) and y (how many chocolates he will select next)—and he uses the data he collects to complete an equation: $4 - x = y$. Or to put it slightly differently, based on his logic, he treats the number of chocolates his opponent takes as an input that, once run through his equation, gives him an output for how many chocolates he himself should take next.

Notice that in the case of our randomness-loving preteen, his Rock, Paper, Scissors strategy didn't really make use of inputs, variables, or outputs. He didn't collect data on what his opponents threw. He didn't have a way to use any data he might have collected. And he didn't have any intentionality behind his gestural output. He just threw whatever he wanted in a vacuum. But boy did he love doing it!

Application

At its core, **application** is simply "understanding where, when, why and how to apply algorithms and which algorithm to apply in a given context," as per the Blueprint. Knowing how to apply an algorithm is just as, if not more, important than knowing how to create one. For example, were the Oxford professor to forget to take one piece of chocolate to begin the game, he might very well end up eating the hot chili. The application of the algorithm requires that it succeed that very crucial first step. Or, sometimes when Tom plays Rock, Paper, Scissors with his son, his son evokes something he calls "light saber." In short, just as Tom is throwing rock or paper or scissors, his son shouts the term, begins making the woo-woo swishing sounds of Luke Skywalker's weapon of choice, and then crushes whatever gesture Tom throws. Tom's algorithm for determining what to throw next cannot be adequately applied to this creative—but illegal, thank you very much—maneuver.

The notion of application also cuts to the core of the issues of ethics that engulf the design and use of algorithms today. Many people are unaware of "where, when, why, and how" algorithms operate in our world. Everything you see in your social media feed streams past you because of many algorithms operating clandestinely beneath the screen. We say algorithms in the plural form because it oversimplifies matters to point a finger at just one company. No one company is in control of our digital lives. Companies share information, plug into each other's systems, and sell our data to myriad other companies. There's a reason the term *big data* has gained so much traction today. Considering the bigness of the data, companies can't possibly make sense of it manually. They have to make sense of it automatically, which means they need a sophisticated logic executing things behind the scenes. That's where algorithms come in. As suggested earlier, the kinds of decisions algorithms make on behalf of companies are becoming increasingly concerning. Should a company's algorithm, which is hidden from our view and opaque even when made available, have the power to determine without human intervention whether a self-driving car stops and slams on the brakes when its sensors detect something that might or might not be a child in the road? Answers to such questions are not easy, which is why all content-area teachers should become familiar with them and ask themselves what algorithms mean for their pedagogy.

In Sum

From chessboards to social media, children's games to campus exhibitions, algorithms are all around us. What is especially powerful about algorithms is that they represent not only a concept, but more accurately, a way of thinking about and acting in the world. That's why reimagining the algorithms in one's content area can be well worth teachers' attention: algorithms offer a way to deepen one's craft. What's more, when teachers and students begin to understand that algorithms are all around us and that they are not the domain of mathematicians and computer scientists alone, we create opportunities for people to think more confidently and critically about the way companies and governments increasingly automate core aspects of life—often in ways that are hidden from public view. It doesn't take much to get started. Just ask yourself how any of the subconcepts earlier could be used in your current teaching and curriculum to deepen existing assignments and learning experiences. We suspect that doing so will quickly demonstrate that computationality has much to offer you and your students. And with that kind of input and curricular variables at your fingertips, the outputs will propel you forward.

Connections to Content Areas

By this point, we hope it is clear that algorithms play such an important role in our world that all teachers and students benefit from understanding their basic nature and function. Still, what is a content-area teacher to do with that information? How does one use the concepts shared earlier to deepen and expand their classroom practice? Well, let's take a look.

English Language Arts

Some literature is inherently algorithmic. Shakespearean sonnets are a great example. Sonnets are composed of fourteen lines that rhyme in a prescribed pattern: ababcdcdefefgg. They also employ various literary devices to convey meaning, like repeating vowel sounds, or assonance. When studying how sonnets work, ELA teachers can focus on the choices poets make as writers within the sonnet algorithm. For example, if line 1 ends with the word *blue* then line 3 cannot end with the word *bird*, even if the author is writing about a blue bird. Similarly, if a poet has to choose a word, she would be wise to look for other words or images she wishes to associate it with and see if she can tighten the association by repeating vowel or consonant sounds. Using algorithms as a guiding framework, the quality of students' analysis—and their own writing of sonnets—can be increased in so many ways.

History

At the heart of studying history is the examination of why human beings and governments made the decisions they made. Similar to studying literature, much of what students must do is to interrogate the decisions others made in hopes that it will teach them how to make better decisions themselves, as writers and as citizens. History teachers might try this: Identify a key decision made by some historical figure. Then, ask students to imagine that the historical figure created a chart for herself that included three columns: inputs, variables, and outcomes. Finally, still imagining themselves to be the historical figure, ask students to fill out the table for some significant historical decision. For instance, what kinds of variables might Harriet Tubman's table have included on when and how to free her family when she returned from Philadelphia to Maryland? What inputs might have informed President Truman's decision to authorize the use of the atomic bomb? These questions encourage deep engagement with historical content—and they happen to be algorithmic.

Science

As mentioned earlier, algorithms can be used to operationalize Boolean logic. Nowhere is that so tangible and electrifying as in exploring circuits. In a unit studying electricity, students might explore the way circuits turn on and off, hypothesizing the logic that dictates when electricity flows. To bring this to life in the classroom, teachers could use a product called Snap Circuits, which gives students opportunities to posit the cause-and-effect relationship between parts of a working circuit. What happens, for example, when electricity flows from batteries and encounters a switch? We can see that depending on the position of the switch, the light indicating electrical flow turns on or off. But why does it do that? How exactly does the switch do that? Such questions naturally uncover opportunities to examine the logic undergirding electrical engineering and computing.

Math

Recall the simple equation we wrote to represent the professor's chocolate and chili game? Well, students can write similar expressions and equations to represent all kinds of decisions they make every day. How do students decide what time to wake up? What route do they take to and from school? How do they determine how much to save for that trip they want to take or a new pair of sneakers? By creating subtle opportunities for students to represent their world algorithmically, teachers can help students see that what they learn in school is hardly contained within the classroom walls. Of course, in its most explicit form, teachers could look at actual examples of algorithms online. Just be careful that they don't have the unintended effect of making students feel computationally inadequate.

The Arts

Music is algorithmic. Depending on the note played at a given moment in a given key of a given piece of music, the note that follows can only likely be a few options. Try playing a piece of music for students. Pause the track before the next note is played. Ask students to vote on what note they think will come next and explain why. Then, extend their thinking by taking the top two options. Ask students to vote on what the next NEXT notes might be. If a Bb is played next, what note do you think would follow that? And so on and so on. By asking students to predict what will come based on what has transpired and asking them to explain their rationale, teachers can create a space where the wonder of algorithmic creativity emerges from the very things we enjoy already.

For Further Exploration

- Watch | BBC documentary on algorithms featuring Oxford math professor Marcus du Sautoy can be found at https://youtu.be/kiFfp-HAu64
- Read | O'Neil, C. (2016). *Weapons of math destruction: How big data increases inequality and threatens democracy.* New York: Crown.
- Read | Williamson, B. (2015). Governing software: Networks, databases and algorithmic power in the digital governance of public education. *Learning, Media and Technology, 40*(1), 83–105.

5 | Programming

The chessboard Tom bought isn't magical, though it is often compared to a bespelled game memorably played at Hogwarts. From the seemingly automated sliding of chess pieces to the way Tom discovered and purchased the board, programming languages operated in the background. Programming languages are mostly invisible, operating at the speed of electricity across complex network infrastructures. Remember that *digital* refers to software and that software is powered by human and computational languages.

To start, in order for the chessboard to work, it must be connected via Bluetooth to a smartphone that has the manufacturer's mobile app. Programming languages power the phone being used, the receiver in the chessboard, and the mobile app itself. You cannot easily see all of those languages. (Notice the plural form of languages we are using here. Any piece of software tends to rely on multiple programming languages at once, even if those who created the software focused their development on a single language.) The programing languages are designed to be hidden, sometimes protected doggedly in the name of intellectual property. So when the average person gets uncomfortable with words like *programming* or *coding*, it makes total sense. You are intentionally shielded from programming languages. Instead, you just see a button or a picture. The thing just works.

Another level of programming languages is at play, though. Remember that Tom purchased the chessboard because he was the focus of a targeted marketing campaign. Yes, he had also imbibed much of a bottle of Cabernet Franc from a region called Samur-Champigny (see how the memories come back with time!), but that alone would not have resulted in his purchasing the chessboard. A complex web of marketing and sales programming languages and systems was also at play. Very likely, Tom's web browser noted his having watched a YouTube video of

Programming

the chessboard and automatically captured that information. The browser and YouTube share owners: Google. Google also operates a marketing juggernaut. It is quite possible that the owners of the chessboard company used Google to cross-reference users' search histories with their Instagram accounts. Again, all of this happens rapidly, invisibly, and automatically. And all of this is made possible because human beings write computer programs to make it happen. When Tom saw the advertisement for the chessboard, it was the culmination of a computational chorus directed to increase the chances that he would do so. It is possible that he was targeted late at night, when anyone on social media tends to exercise poorer judgement than in the morning. And maybe the marketing system knew he had purchased copious amounts of wine that evening. Tom used his phone to pay for wine at the store.

If, as the Blueprint team says, programming "is about giving instructions to computers ... [and] can be done through a constantly changing set of languages," how is the average teacher supposed to get more familiar with it? All the languages seem hidden! There is no shortage of tools teachers can use to become more familiar with computer code, some of which we will explore here. But you can also expose the code that already comprises your daily life. The easiest way to do so is to navigate to a favorite website you visit every day. On any web page, you can right click on the screen and see an option to "View Source." (If you don't see this option, just search online for "view source" and your type of computer and browser.) A new tab will open that shows you the Hypertext Markup Language (HTML) language that computers use to put that web page together. Websites often use three main languages: HTML, Cascading Style Sheets (CSS), and JavaScript. When you look at the HTML code for a favorite website, just remember that a team of human beings wrote what you see in order to tell a computer how to create the web page. You experience programming every day. You just might not know where to see it.

▎ Talking and Dancing with Robots

Allow us to begin with a tale of two computer science (CS) learning environments. The first is a story about Excel. Gerald's doctoral program required that he participate in two 4-hour workshops featuring Excel in order to support the collection and analysis of data. The workshop was conducted in a typical university computer lab, with rows of tables containing desktop computers. The instructor provided a very detailed workbook on the functionality of Excel and then proceeded to walk students through it, menu item (File > New) by menu item (Help > Help). Gerald and his fellow students were expected to follow along, step by step, in exactly the order prescribed by the instructor and his workbook. They worked hard to follow the instructions, but found that they had questions and scenarios that ranged beyond the skills being addressed at any one time, and students experienced an unnecessary disconnect between the instruction provided and their own needs and interests. While Gerald's knowledge of Excel certainly increased as a result of the workshop, he noticed that his role as a learner had shifted. Rather than feeling free to explore and try things out on his own, to ask questions shaped by his own interests and the needs of his research, he was encouraged to simply be compliant as a learner and get with the program.

It is certain that this demotivation was an unintended outcome of this type of learning environment. The instructor certainly wanted his students to learn Excel. He was likely doing what he had done in the past and what probably worked in meeting his own learning style and goals. However, the relationship between a teacher-centered, low-autonomy, supportive learning environment and low levels of engagement and motivation stuck with Gerald and ended up shaping his own teaching.

The second story involves a cat. When Gerald was a middle school science teacher, his fifth-grade colleagues asked him to introduce their students to Scratch. Scratch was created by the Lifelong Kindergarten group at the Massachusetts Institute of Technology. It was designed as a tool to allow young people to explore coding in a fun and friendly way. The mantra of these designers was "low floor, no ceiling," meaning that it should be easy for anyone to get started in Scratch; what was possible in terms of complexity was determined by the learner, not the tool (see Figure 5.1).

Scratch utilizes block-based programming, meaning that one creates programs in Scratch by snapping blocks together (similar to Turtle Blocks in Chapter 3). The fifth-grade teachers very much wanted their students to have an experience of Scratch, but were not comfortable providing the instruction themselves. For these teachers, and for most if not all of their students, this would be their first experience with coding of any sort.

Gerald's original plan was to create a series of learning cycles where students would be introduced to a set of functionalities in Scratch and then practice it on their own through structured (meaning, teacher-designed) activities. The first cycle was to feature some basic skills: adding/modifying sprites (sprites refer to cartoonish characters), using speech and thought bubbles and movement.

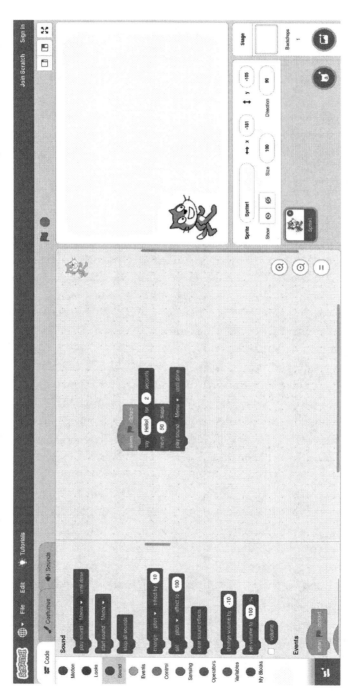

Figure 5.1 Introductory project demonstrating basic functionality in Scratch.

There are three basic components of the Scratch user interface. On the left are categories of blocks represented by different colors; the blocks for the sound category are highlighted. These blocks are dragged into the middle portion of the screen to create the program itself. In what you see, a program instructs Scratchy the cat (the default sprite) to use a speech bubble to say "hello" for two seconds (*say*), then *move* fifty steps across the screen, and then meow (*play sound*)- all once the green flag is pressed. On the right is where the program is "performed."

Gerald has used this program as an introduction to Scratch for years, for both children and adults. Not once has an audience not laughed when the cat meows. Not once. This joy at the surprise tends to lead new Scratchers to try out all kinds of sounds. Scratch features a pretty extensive sound library, along with the functionality to both edit and record sounds. (We leave it to you to imagine just what other sounds participants have recorded over the years!)

In the fifth-grade classroom, students were seated at tables with their own laptops, while Gerald demonstrated his introductory Scratch program via a Smart Board. Rather than the traditional and orderly pedagogical rhythm of skill–practice–repeat like Gerald experienced in his Excel workshop, something very unexpected took place. As soon as Gerald demonstrated any skill, students tried it out immediately and went on just trying out other blocks to see what they did. They didn't need to wait until the next structured cycle to learn something new. They were ready and eager to just dive in.

Gerald also noticed that as soon as students got something to work, they simply *had* to share with the others around them what they had done and how it worked. Rather than sitting patiently doing only what was asked, students immediately began playing with various blocks and sequences of blocks and then sharing what they had learned—and even what had failed—with one another. They literally popped out of their seats and moved around the room. Gerald and the teachers began to refer to this phenomenon as "The Ripple."

Rather than stop The Ripple, Gerald changed gears. Instead of the organized presentation he had prepared, he started moving from table to table, conferring with students to see what they were trying to accomplish, supporting them in what their next steps could be. If students had mastered a skill, he deputized them to teach it to another student who was ready to learn it. He supported their sharing, their experimentation, and their enthusiasm. Gerald met them where they were and empowered them to move one another along to bigger and more complex things. The entire classroom learning environment shifted from being primarily *teacher-centered* to being primarily *student-centered*. To Gerald, it felt like magic.

Despite the seeming chaos of the experience, Gerald and the other teachers noticed that students were heavily engaged and invested in what they were learning. Their acquisition of new skills was much more iterative than linear. It took students very little time to begin to be able to work on projects of real complexity, such as games or elaborate animations. A pedagogy of exploration, discovery, and sharing arose organically to meet the needs and interests of these students. Student autonomy and engagement were key.

What's great about Scratch is that in addition to empowering students to create animated cats, it increasingly serves as an introductory coding language, one that other companies use to power their computational products. Robotics is a great example. Robotics companies have often either used Scratch to serve as the coding language to program children's robots or emulated Scratch's interface and concepts. In short, when you start with Scratch, you can continue to explore computationality without having to start from scratch. (Get it? *With* and *from*, *Scratch* and *scratch* . . . OK. Moving on!)

A Tale of Two Robotics Projects

We, your authors, have all used robots as vehicles to introduce novices to software programming. The work described in this chapter was inspired by two such robotics projects: one conducted with sixth-grade math and science students, the other conducted with high school students in grades 10 to 12. (We will also hear about Pam's more humanistic robotics project in Chapter 7.)

Why Robots?

In our various experiences with introducing students to programming, we have found that many of them relate differently, and sometimes more positively, to a physical object rather than a digital one. Robots provide the combination of physical and digital experience that seems to be a sweet spot for young people.

As described in Chapter 3, we think of it in terms of abstraction. When older elementary or younger middle school students are working to program digital objects, there is always a moment when the object being programmed is beyond the student's world, "out there" somewhere. This becomes especially relevant when something is not working as intended. Later, students learn the term "debugging," but early in the process they just say, "It's not working!" When encouraged to describe the problem, they often use opaque language: "Scratchy the cat won't meow when I want him to!"

With robots, this process is far less abstract. In the robotics projects that Gerald developed, one of the earliest challenges he gives to students working with robots for the first time is some version of a race. To meet this challenge, students must program the robot to travel, as quickly as possible, in a straight line—say, down a hallway—and then come back again. When they see that their robot is not doing what they intended it to do, meaning their program does not work properly, the robot's physicality seems to reduce the level of abstraction with which they are dealing. When something is not working, their descriptions are far more concrete. Instead of "my robot is not doing what it's supposed to do," they say, "I want the robot to turn right for three seconds, but it's not doing that." Students pick up the robot. They look at it. They then look at the code. Their work is no longer about coding for its own sake. Rather, it is about discovering how to realize one's intention for and with this physical device. Students want the robot—that physical metal thing right over there—to actually behave the way they want it to. We have seen this difference to be a profound one for secondary students.

(As an aside, there is also something about the process of physically assembling their robots that is similarly meaningful to students. Robots often come unassembled, and each time Gerald has begun a robotics project with either middle or high school students, he has them assemble their robots themselves. This process takes about twenty to thirty minutes. During that time, a small transformation takes place in which students form a relationship with the device, often naming their robot whether asked to or not. This experience powerfully, and concretely, sets the stage for the coding work that follows.)

This relationship with the physical robot does not end after the assembly process, either. Gerald remembers one illustrative story fondly. Midway through a robotics project with high school students, groups were given an expansion pack for their robots, which allowed them to add a servo (a mechanism for adding movement) and an external light-emitting diode (LED) light panel to their robots. This is one of the nice features of the robots used, which were called mBots. They are designed for additional construction, like their counterparts from LEGO called LEGO Mindstorms.

Most students added these new components by building the robot up. In such cases, the servo allowed the cross pieces to spin, and the extra LED panel allowed for another set of really bright lights. The robot was no longer just confined to its initial construction. Students literally caused their robots to grow upward.

While most students utilized this type of vertical construction, one student realized that he could use the extra LED panel to add undercarriage lights, like those he had seen in souped-up cars in his neighborhood. This idea really captivated him, and he was determined to realize it. Implementing this idea, though, required the student to disassemble his robot and rebuild it. Gerald explained the extra work involved, but it became obvious that this modification was personally meaningful to the student. He spent almost an entire two-hour session getting this robot and its new undercarriage lighting system to work exactly the way he wanted. This enhanced lighting became a key component later in the project, when the student and his partner incorporated this unique lighting system into a dance they had programmed their robot to perform. The outcomes in terms of both enhanced functionality and student ownership more than justified the time it took for this student to re-engineer his robot. It is hard to imagine this student feeling so interested in and committed to a cat he had coded to meow.

Some Robot and Software Suggestions

There are many robot kits available for classroom use. Dash robots and Ozobots are designed for early elementary students and classrooms. The robots themselves are designed to be fun and inviting. Their programming languages are visual and intuitive in order to meet the needs and skills of pre-readers or early readers. LEGO We Do robots can do more complex things and have a Scratch-like programming language. We have extensive experience working with mBots and LEGO Mindstorms and will discuss them in greater detail in order to identify some key ideas and elements for using them to teach programming to K–12 students.

When designing a robotics project, we have found it useful to consider a set of factors. Price is important, given that particularly in a school setting money is a limited resource. Durability is also important. Ideally, the robots you decide to use should be able to take the wear and tear inflicted by novice users. Degree of difficulty in use and assembly is also very important. The robot should be easy to assemble, store, and expand. Most robot systems, like the mBots and LEGO Mindstorms used in these two projects, come with additional construction parts and sensors so that the robots can be modified for different learning experiences. Further, it is important to consider the logistics necessary to operationalize your robotics program. How will the parts be stored and where? How will you and the students keep track of them? What are the practices and routines around all of these activities in your classroom?

Lastly, robots are programmed using software (formally, software development environments) on a computer or mobile device. Care should be taken in making sure that the software is appropriate for your students developmentally and in terms of the devices and technical support available in your setting. For example, the sixth-grade robotics program Gerald helped design used LEGO Mindstorms with its accompanying software. The high school STEM (science technology engineering, math) enrichment programs that Gerald has designed and led use the mBot along with its Makeblock software. The next section describes the LEGO Mindstorms robots and their Mindstorms software development environment as well as the mBots and their Makeblock software development environment in some detail.

LEGO Mindstorms

LEGO Mindstorms are robot kits that are an extension of the LEGO building ecosystem (see Figure 5.2). The kits include motors, gears, sensors, and other robotic parts and allow for additional construction using LEGO blocks. As such, these robot kits benefit from being already somewhat familiar to most students.

Like Scratch, LEGO Mindstorms software features a block-based programming environment, with blocks that are laid out horizontally instead of vertically. Additionally, clicking on a block reveals the options available for that block. For example, clicking on a motor block will reveal options for the amount of power and direction. A simple program might utilize three types of Mindstorms blocks: *play*, *display*, and *make sound*. In this program, once the *play* button is pressed, the

Figure 5.2 LEGO Mindstorms robot used with the sixth-grade program.

software program is initiated and the word "Hello" is displayed as text on the robot's screen and a tone is played through its speaker. In the Mindstorms software development environment, clicking on a block reveals the various options available for that block. For example, the *display* block offers the options of text, shapes, or images.

The mBot

The mBot is an affordable (about $100) robot that comes with two motors and several sensors (ultrasound, light, and line), and on-board LEDs (see Figure 5.3). As described earlier, extension packs are available that add functionality, like building kits, sensor kits, and lighting kits. mBots are relatively easy to assemble and come with clear, graphical directions.

mBots are programmed using the Makeblock software development environment, which is based on Scratch. As with Scratch, the Makeblock user interface is divided into sections. On the left, the user selects the device (in this case, the mBot). In the center are the programming blocks divided into various categories. On the right is the program we are building. The resultant program would ultimately get uploaded to the mBot (see Figure 5.4).

Like the Mindstorms code depicted earlier, this program uses a small set of blocks: *LED, play note, forever,* and *wait*. The code lights up the LED in pink while playing a C4 tone for a quarter note, waits a second, then lights up the LED in blue while playing an F2 tone for a quarter note. These blocks are embedded

Figure 5.3 The mBot.

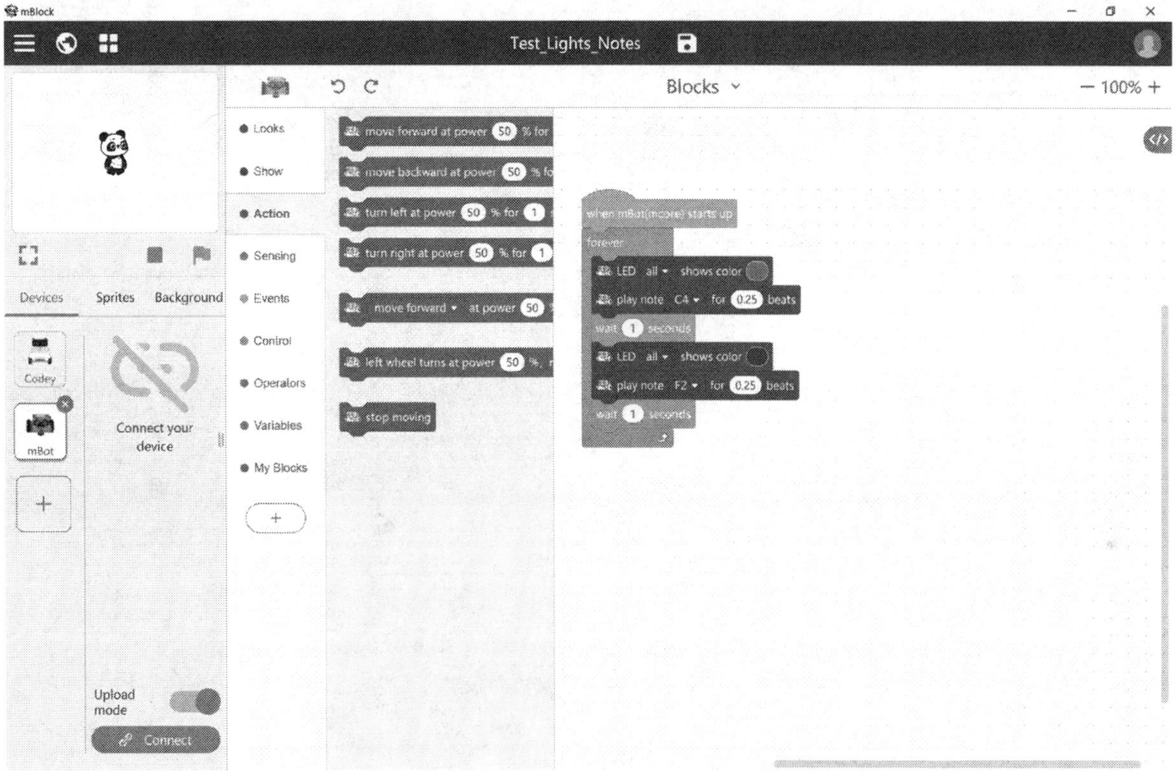

Figure 5.4 A program for the mBot that blinks its LEDs on and off while playing sound.

within the forever block, which means the robot will do this over and over again as long as it is powered up.

One last feature of mBot's Makeblock software is the ability for users to move beyond block-based programming to true text-based programming. In our experience, this is not something that all students will want, but for those who do the ability to make this transition is an important feature. Some students like the ability to program quickly by editing the text instead of being solely tied to blocks. While most introductory-level students will not be ready for text-based coding of their robots, some might be. And in our experience, many are eager to know what is going on "under the hood" even if they are not ready to make use of this text-based coding yet. Makeblock lets them see it, and even edit if they feel ready (see Figure 5.5).

We will not review this text-based code in detail here, but invite you to try to connect what you see in the text to the blocks on the left. Gerald has done this type of exercise with students, even young adolescent students (as described in Chapter 3). In doing so, he has found that as students try to make connections, the degree of abstraction with text-based code begins to dissipate and the code becomes more readable.

Some Best Practices for Teaching with Robots

Our work with robotics had led us to discover some best practices. These have been test-driven with students in grades K–12 in various settings and with various robots.

Pedagogy and Curriculum Design

The first element is the learning environment in which this work takes place. Both the high school and sixth-grade robotics projects shared a similar pedagogy and curriculum design, which consisted of three main elements: a student-centered learning environment, authentic student work, and programming. Allow us to share a brief overview of each. First, we aim for student-centered learning environments. Students had a great deal of say in terms of how they worked with their partners and how they managed their own time. They were presented with open-ended challenges that were designed to allow them to demonstrate their proficiency as programmers, while allowing them to pursue their own interests and ways of working together. The teachers in these two projects acted as facilitators

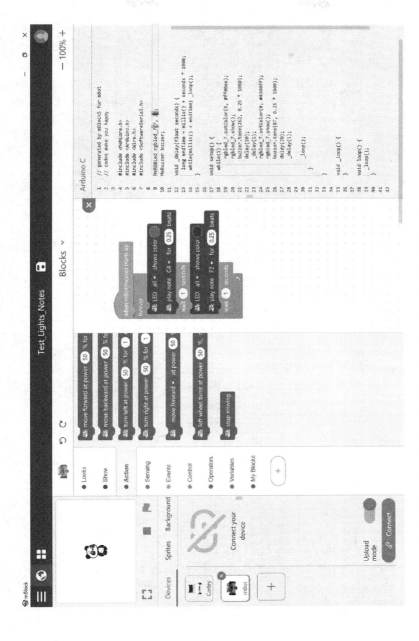

Figure 5.5 Makeblock interface showing block-based and text-based coding side by side.

and mentors to the students, rather than as the sole sources of all knowledge and skills. Second, we value authentic student work. Various challenges that Gerald included in these projects, such as a Dance-Off Challenge (see later), where groups of students programmed their robots to dance to a song of their own choosing. We aim for a strategic mixture of fun, challenge, and choice so that students will take ownership (and even pleasure) in completing the projects. The result is, we hope, a sense of authenticity and joy. Finally, these projects were designed to teach the core CS concept of programming, which we think in terms of what it means to use visual and text-based languages to communicate with computers.

Two Examples of Robotics Projects

Now let's dive into how these design principles, pedagogical elements, and curriculum came together in two specific robotics projects.

Example 1: A Sixth-Grade Math/Science Robotics Project
When Gerald was a middle school science teacher, one of his sixth-grade colleagues, Lauren, was interested in developing a robotics program for her math students. Her goal was to both increase some of their math skills, particularly in the areas of algebra and geometry, while also improving their collaboration skills. Lauren had already arranged a grant for the LEGO Mindstorms robots and had them in her classroom. She also had the Mindstorms software development environment installed on her classroom set of computers.

The curriculum that Lauren and Gerald developed was organized around a series of increasingly complex challenges that students worked in groups to meet. Here were the challenges. They called the first one the Boat Float. This was not a robotics challenge, but was a warm-up engineering/collaboration task where the student groups were given paper, foil, Post-its, and pennies and charged with designing and building a boat that could hold the largest numbers of pennies. (Notice how concrete and tangible this is!) Next, Gerald and Lauren orchestrated a Robot Race. For this challenge, the student groups were tasked with assembling their Mindstorms robots and programming them to run (as fast as possible, of course) down a 100-foot hallway, then turn around and race back to the starting point. It was during this challenge that the students were introduced to the Mindstorms software development environment. At the end of this challenge, student groups demonstrated their robots actually racing. Finally, it was time for the Dance-Off Challenge. For this challenge, student groups were tasked with reassembling their robots to include a sensor (light sensor, sound sensor, or touch sensor) and then to create a program that had their robots dance to a song of the group's choosing. Students had to add the sensor functionality to their programs, specifically taking information from the sensor to trigger a behavior in the robot. For example, using the sound sensor, students could program their robots to start their dance by clapping their hands. Students demonstrated their dancing robots on a classroom dance floor.

Pedagogically, this project sequence was consistent with Gerald's Scratch project described earlier, with students being allowed to explore the basic functionality of programming their robots and then working together to design and implement solutions to the various challenges. This part in particular was important to Lauren, as one of her main goals was to increase her students' capacity to collaborate with one another. Her sixth-graders spent about forty-five minutes per day over the course of six weeks engaged in this robotics program. During that time, students were asked to keep a journal that captured both their daily progress in building and programming, as well as the ways their groups collaborated successfully or not.

Example 2: A High School Robotics STEM Enrichment Program
For several years, Gerald has worked with a nonprofit organization in Mt. Vernon, New York, which focuses on improving educational outcomes for students in grades 4–12 by providing STEM enrichment programs of all types (e.g., math tutoring, coding, and robotics) throughout the school year and the summer. During one of those years, Gerald was approached to offer a Saturday STEM enrichment program for high school students that focused on programming robots. This program took place in two-and-half-hour sessions over six consecutive Saturdays. As with Lauren's sixth-grade robotics program, Gerald's robotics program for the high school students was also designed around an increasingly complex series of challenges. And, as we might expect, the pedagogy employed was also similar.

The STEM enrichment program provided several opportunities that are not easily achieved in a K–12 school setting. First, there was a small number of students. Approximately twenty-five tenth, eleventh, and twelfth graders self-selected to participate. Second, while this enrichment program had clear curricular goals and learning objectives, the extracurricular nature of the program facilitated Gerald's being able to customize the work to students' individual interests. For example, one team was interested in the dance that bees do to inform their hive mates of the location of nectar and so worked to program their robot to perform that kind of dance. And they could do so, in part, because we weren't beholden strictly to a scope and sequence.

Programming

Here was the curriculum that Gerald and his team designed for these high school students. Students were grouped in pairs, given their mBots, and tasked with assembling them. We began with the basics. Students worked in their pairs to assemble their robots (and, of course, name them), and then create their first programs. These start with the flashing LEDs and playing sound programs, as depicted in Figure 5.5 and then go from there. Next, we created an Obstacle Course project. Once the students had successfully learned the basics of programming their mBots, they were tasked with writing a program that allowed their mBot to navigate through an obstacle course. This challenge required them to add sensing functionality to their robots, typically using the ultrasound sensor that the robot used to judge distance. The sensors provided information about the environment (such as proximity to an object), which would then automatically change the robot's behavior. Finally, students were ready for the Dance-Off Challenge. This challenge is the same as it was for the sixth-grade students. The pairs worked to program their robots to dance for at least two minutes to a song of their own choosing. Once again, they exhibited their work via a classroom dance floor.

We have seen other sets of students and teachers do other really great things with robots of all kinds, and probably you have too. You're limited only by your imagination. But now let's step back for a moment and unpack the subconcepts that are at play.

Uncovering Subconcepts

This chapter has focused on the key concept of programming, including its subconcepts languages, syntax, development environments, and collaboration. Each of these has been illustrated in the description of Gerald's robotics work with students as described earlier. (By now you might see, too, that much of this discussion can apply to Gerald's interactive machines project with seventh-grade science students in Chapter 3 as well.) Let's look at how each of the subconcepts played out.

Languages

In these robotics examples, we have seen students work with two block-based coding **languages**: Makeblock (for the mBot) and LEGO Mindstorms. According to the Blueprint, languages is defined thus: "Programming languages have different applications and require different amounts of prior knowledge." Each has its own syntax and development environment, along with particular affordances, all of which have an important effect on students' learning.

Syntax

Here is what the NYC DOE Blueprint has to say about **syntax**: "All programming languages have a set of commands or reserved words and grammar rules that must be followed." Both Mindstorms and Makeblock are block-based programming languages that use conventions to determine how the programmer can operate within its software development environment. For example, Mindstorms requires that programs are built horizontally, whereas Makeblock requires that programs are built vertically. Each language has conventions as well for ensuring that programmers use the appropriate syntax. Makeblock, like its progenitor Scratch, uses the convention of shape that must be locked together in certain ways. Blocks that don't work together won't fit together.

In Figure 5.6, for instance, the *LED* and *wait* blocks will fit into the *repeat* block, but the *pick random* block will not. The *pick random* block is about selecting a range of numbers, so it fits into the parts of blocks where numbers would go. For example, if we want our program to have a pause which could range from one to ten seconds, we could slide the *pick random* block into the circle (which currently contains a "1") on the *wait* block. Mindstorms, on the other hand, allows every brick to connect to every other brick. It uses a different convention to enforce effective programming. The user must properly assign values to options for the various blocks in order to have their program work as intended. In this sample program, the robot plays the sound file "Hello" three times and then drives its large motor to turn ten rotations. Then it stops. The success or failure of the program is determined not by the shape of the blocks, but rather by the productive use of the various options available for each block. The repeat block has a count option (we chose "3"). The sound block has options for file selection (we chose "Hello"), volume (we chose "100%"), and play type (we choose once). This group of blocks results in the sound "Hello" being played three times in a row by the robot. Then the action block controlling the large motor has options for power (we chose "50%"), rotations (we chose "10"), and brake at end (we choose "True"). When added to the repeat block, this action block has the robot move forward by having the motor complete ten rotations at 50% power once the robot

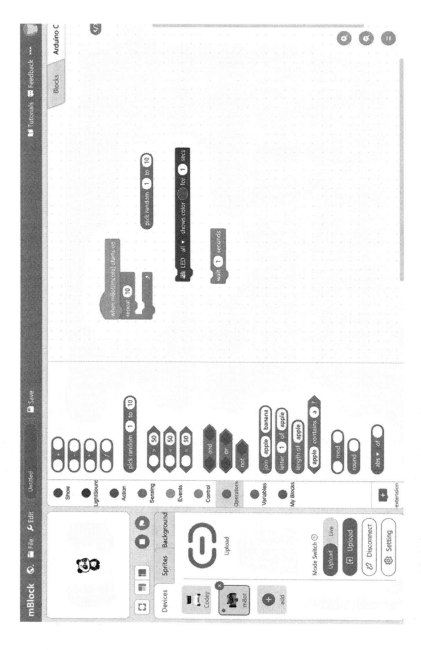

Figure 5.6 Block shape as syntax in the Makeblock software development environment.

has played "Hello" three times in a row. In the Mindstorms software development environment, block options—not shapes, as in Scratch—are everything.

Development Environments

In these two robotics projects, we saw students working with two different **development environments**, which the NYC DOE Blueprint defines thus: "Programmers use development environments to create applications; these environments have an editor to write code, run and show a program's output and log errors that arise." Development environments are to programming what Microsoft Word and Google Docs are to writing. Both development environments described in this chapter—namely the Makeblock environment for the mBots and the LEGO Mindstorms software—are block-based and allow students to make and test the code for their robots. One of the things that ends up being important in these types of robotics experiences is students coming to understand the conventions of the development environments. Both Makeblock and Mindstorms group their programming blocks into color-coded categories, and both have conventions for indicating the options associated with specific blocks. Students learn to interpret which functionality is contained within each of these categories, as well as how the different sets of blocks work in order to use the software correctly and efficiently.

Collaboration

In both the sixth-grade robotics project and the high school STEM enrichment program, teachers explicitly used this work to enhance their students' ability to collaborate productively with one another. Here is what the NYC DOE Blueprint has to say about **collaboration**: "Collaborating on code is complex because each line is part of a larger algorithm or abstraction. Clearly setting team roles, saving versions along the way, and using parallel versions are some ways to manage the complexity." We have found that robots provide a unique opportunity for students to do programming work that is meaningful and authentic to them. They are honestly engaged by the challenges involved in first assembling and then programming the robots to do their bidding. We have found (as have many other teachers) that these challenges are enhanced by collaboration, allowing a team solution rather than just an individual one.

Additionally, there can be a multiplicative effect to this type of collaboration. In the projects in which Gerald has been involved, he works to celebrate the accomplishments of individual teams by calling out a clever solution to a challenge: "If you really want to be impressed, take a look at what Group 2 has done!" This is very empowering to groups and encourages knowledge and skill sharing across teams. We have found this type of strategy to be extremely effective in both enhancing the development of CS skills and concepts, but also through building a learning environment that fosters, supports, and promotes critical thinking and problem solving.

 ## In Sum

This chapter has focused on the CS concept of programming and its subconcepts of languages, syntax, development environments, and collaboration. In addition, this chapter explored a connection to pedagogical strategies that can be used by teachers at all grade levels and with all different levels of experience to successfully orchestrate curricular projects that include the use of programming. There is clearly a place for formal CS education in secondary school settings, like AP Computer Science and coding electives. For most students and school settings, however, this structure is neither viable nor desirable. Not every student is interested in this type of formal CS education, and not all teachers are trained to teach with the required depth.

Therefore, we are strong proponents of embedding CS skills and concepts into existing content areas, like programming robots in increasingly fun and complex ways. Students of all ranges of ability and experience can deeply engage in their content area, and can do work that is both computational and meaningful.

 ## Connections to Content Areas

While the CS skill of *programming* may seem narrow one, we have found it to be a very broad and useful skill across various content areas.

English Language Arts

Tom and Gerald have developed a project they call BardBots, which, as the name implies, combines programming with the study of Shakespeare. The project

Programming

emerged over a series of conversations where we started thinking creatively about computer science education: What does literary study teach us about computational thinking? What does robotics teach us about humanity? Are computational languages really just another kind of human language? Over the course of the BardBots project, students work in groups to do the following: closely read a scene from Shakespeare, plot stage directions for their scene, program robots to "perform" the scene, and complete Babble Logs—critical reflections about the relationship between human and computational languages. (And wait until you read about Pam's adaptation of BardBots in Chapter 7!)

History

Tom has put together a really cool project that he calls *States of Education*. This project is an interactive map that allows users to click on a state and then see the portion of that state's constitution that discusses the right to a public education (see Figure 5.7).

Tom coded this project using the R programming language, which can be used to create all sorts of data visualizations. History teachers and students, by starting with his code and then modifying it to focus on other areas of interest,

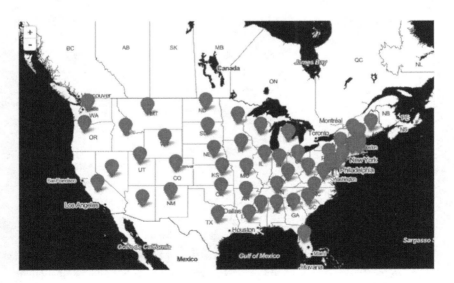

Figure 5.7 Tom's project *States of Education*.

89

could easily use Tom's model to analyze other kinds of primary and secondary source artifacts.

Science

In Chapter 3 we described in detail a program Gerald designed for his former seventh-grade students that worked to have them deepen their understanding of feedback mechanisms by building an interactive device. This type of project could be implemented in any one of a variety of programming languages, from block-based ones like Scratch or Turtle Blocks, to text-based ones like Python or R. Additionally, while Gerald's project focused on feedback mechanisms as a key concept, similar projects could be designed and implemented that make use of modeling in science classrooms, a strategy that has a deep and compelling research base. Students, for example, could model all sorts of scientific concepts: predator–prey relationships, weather patterns, the growth of plants, the causes of earthquakes, enzyme activity, and forces and motion.

Math

Programming and robotics projects can be used to enhance the acquisition and application of math skills across grade levels in a variety of ways. For example, programming directly addresses the development of sequential thinking, which is essential for the deep understanding of math. Recall the Robot Race challenge, where students had to get their robots to roll straight down a hallway, turn 180 degrees, and return down the hallway. Breaking down these steps becomes an essential component of writing the necessary software programs that get the robots to race successfully. Or consider how algebraic skills such as variables and functions are incorporated into programming projects. Working with sensors necessitates the establishment of a variable (such as sound level), which can then be used to trigger other events in the program. Functions emphasize the subconcept of modularity, in which individual instructions can be built once and then are easily reused. Both of these skills became critical elements of the Dance-Off Challenge. Finally, robots and programming can be used to focus on even more basic math skills. For example, students can be asked to program their robots to "perform" increasingly complex shapes, starting with the simplest (squares) and then progressing to those that are more complex (stars). Solving these challenges enhances student understanding of geometric relationships. (See Chapter 3.)

The Arts

Processing is a programming language that was created to allow noncoders to generate images of all kinds. The code is easily readable by people and can be used to teach both coding and the various components of geometric shapes, as well as their relationships to one another. This type of tool has all kinds of implications for uses in art classes and projects across grade levels. *Processing* can create and manipulate shapes; can define colors, hues, and shades; and can be used to create interactive graphics of various types. There are also myriad examples available online.

 For Further Exploration

- Explore | Scratch: https://scratch.mit.edu/
- Explore | mBots: https://www.makeblock.com/steam-kits/mbot
- Play with | LEGO Mindstorms: https://www.lego.com/en-us/product/lego-mindstorms-ev3-31313
- Dabble in | Processing: https://processing.org/

6 | Data

When the chessboard arrived at Tom's apartment a few days after Thanksgiving, you can imagine the level of anticipation that had built up. Was it the best decision he had ever made in life? No. Was it the worst? Not by a longshot. And there was no way he was turning back. As he carried the box up four flights of stairs to his family's tiny apartment, Tom believed that it contained not only a chessboard but the possibility for redemption. If it was as phenomenal as it appeared to be, no one would question his decision to buy it. His impulsiveness would instantly transform into a mark of foresight and innovation.

He carefully opened the box with his wife and son huddled over watching. The board was glorious, heavier and bigger than he expected because it contained inside a series of electromagnetic rods that powered the movement of the pieces. Then he opened the smaller boxes with the pieces. Disappointment followed. A single pawn was missing. To be clear, these pieces were meticulously wrapped in such a way that there was no possibility anything loosened or fell out. Whoever packed the box just forgot a pawn. Getting a chessboard with a missing pawn is like getting a car with three tires. It is useless.

In a moment of sheer indignation, Tom took a picture of the chessboard with the missing pawn and sent a message via Twitter to the company. He did the same on Instagram. Probably on Facebook and any other service he could find, but he was seeing red at that point so his actions get fuzzy.

What does this have to do with data? The Blueprint says the following about data: "Computers can be used to collect, store and analyze massive amounts of data quickly and reliably. Computer programs can use data to make decisions or to automate tasks." Doubtless, data are used to power the chessboard, from how the electromagnets operate to the moves that the machine makes, to the way it connects players on other sides of the world.

But perhaps more familiar, yet less well known, is the way computers collect, store, manipulate, and act on data all the time.

Consider the picture of the missing pawn Tom snapped and blasted over social media.

Like any picture taken with a smartphone, the picture contained over one hundred kinds of data that are attached to it called metadata. The single picture of the missing pawn included the type of phone, operating system, longitude and latitude of where it was taken, camera lens type, and even the direction the person taking the picture was facing. That information comes standard with the photograph. It does not include other data that social media companies can associate with the photo, which gets added to the photo online. For example, let's say you post a photo on social media that features you posing with your chessboard and your best friend. When you post the photo online, social media companies increasingly use it to generate more associated data. They can automatically identify who else is in your photo and suggest that you "tag" them. Companies can also ask you to confirm that you are in a specific geographic location. They then monitor who you share it with, who likes it, who comments, and so on. Companies take all those data and they use them to create a profile of you as a user: your interests and aversions, your closest friends, and your behaviors. Those data are used to market products and services to you, like the greatest chessboard ever created.

Plotting Plots in Chinatown

There is something to be said for getting lost in one's own town. The navigation app on Tom's phone said the trip would take forty minutes. He left over an hour ahead of time. Walking through the pre-dawn familiar streets to the subway, he boarded the D train at 125th Street and was whipped along to his destination in plenty of time. Disembarking at Grand Street, Tom had time to spare. So he sat on a bench in the station and read the last chapter in an unfinished novel for his book club.

Checking his watch, Tom hurried upstairs ready to walk the couple of blocks to the high school where he was scheduled to run a morning workshop. As he emerged at street level, though, he was struck by what can only be described as a linguistic hit-and-run. A man was yelling (Tom assumed at him) in a language Tom didn't understand. As he looked around, Tom's eyes were knocked into a state of alphabetic disorientation, the sweeping calligraphy of unfamiliar

Data

characters seemed to be everywhere. He began walking briskly now, as you can imagine, in the direction where he believed the school to be. After a few blocks, Tom realized he hadn't recognized English words anywhere. While the street signs were bilingual, the presence of English was overshadowed by the sheer dominance of Mandarin.

Chinatown was not Tom's intended destination, but the school was in a part of Manhattan where several neighborhoods overlap. Lower Manhattan predates the neat and tidy grid system that defines the island north of 14th Street. The East Village, the Lower East Side, Chinatown, Little Italy—they all blur together. Tom was in old Manhattan. Old, as in streets crisscross illogically, confusing invading British troops. Old, like that's the spot where Boss Tweed rigged elections. Old, like centuries of stories of war and corruption and ambition and hope and love—and the myriad dialects and languages in which such stories were told.

Tom found the entrance to the school. The security guard commented on his ensemble, noting Tom's light blue shirt and dark blue pants resembled her own uniform. Tom smiled, raised his foot in the air, and asked if his polished brown leather shoes with red laces are standard issue for school safety officers. The officer laughed, also a believer in the power of unexpected bursts of color in the world. Navigating the halls, Tom huffed up the stairs and was soon standing before a group of ten teachers, mostly English language arts (ELA), but also special education, math, and physics. Apparently, the title of the workshop attracted a respectable interdisciplinary crowd: "An Introduction to Integrating Computer Science into ELA."

Tom began his workshop with a picture. It was an image of the gates of Columbia University at 116th Street and Broadway in New York. As you observe the gateway, which is referred to as College Walk, there are two statues flanking the entrance to campus. On the left, there is a male figure wearing a robe, his bare chest exposed for all to see. He holds an orb. He is labeled "Sciences." On the right, there is a female figure wearing a fuller robe. She holds an open book, pages facing out. She is called "Letters." Tom used this image as a way to introduce the idea that, for centuries, we have confidently separated the sciences from the language arts. The result is that computational methods become the expertise area of STEM professionals whose titles denote science, technology, engineering, or math. The problem with that, recall, is the value of computer science in K–12 spaces is not in the least bit limited to STEM subjects. We do not limit the value of reading and writing to English class, do we? Of course not. That's because we understand that the use of language to consume and produce texts transcends all disciplines. Similarly, we must not limit the value of computational methods to a subset of disciplines that evoke the image of bare-chested men holding orbs over Broadway.

In Chinatown that morning, the teachers' interest in the workshop flowed, in part, from Computer Science for All (CS4All). Recall from Chapter 1 that in 2014, the Obama administration launched CS4All as a nationwide program, kicking it off with a press event in which the president learned to write a simple computer program with students at the White House. He was hailed as the Coder in Chief. CS4All was not strictly a federal initiative, per se. Instead, it consisted of a network of public, private, and philanthropic partners who joined forces to promote computer science education in K–12 schools. President Obama's photo op was just one piece. In addition, companies like Google, Amazon, Facebook, and Microsoft all supported raising awareness of computer science in K–12 schools. Philanthropists like Fred Wilson, the venture capitalist behind Union Square Ventures, worked with elected officials to support public schools in the New York City at scale. Wilson funded the establishment of two high schools in New York— one in Manhattan, another in the Bronx—that made software engineering a core part of their vision. With broad support, New York mayor Bill de Blasio launched the city's own CS4All campaign, providing curricular resources and incentives for schools to step up their computer science offerings. All that buzz likely lured teachers to Tom's workshop that morning.

"Our goal today is to walk between those two statues flanking the entrance to College Walk," Tom began, pointing at the picture of Columbia. "Computer science is not the domain of STEM. In fact, it can be employed very meaningfully in the humanities as well. Rather than treat computer science as a discipline in its own right, I want to share with you how computational methods can be used to deepen and expand the ways you already teach (or were taught) literature."

Deepen and expand content-area instruction. For Tom, that is an oft-repeated phrase. When teachers stop thinking about computer science as a circumscribed discipline and begin thinking in terms of computational methods that can be adapted for the work they already do, pedagogical paradigms shift.

"How many of you have read (or were supposed to have read) Shakespeare's *Romeo and Juliet*?" All hands shot up. "Excellent," Tom went on, "so you all have a general recollection of the story. Well, let me share with you an assessment question similar to the ones you might have encountered in a middle or high school English class." On the screen flashed a prompt: *How does Shakespeare portray the relationship between love and death in Romeo and Juliet*? The question seemed straightforward enough. Reading the room, Tom said, "By the looks on your faces,

Data

Table 6.1 The Frequency of the Words "Love" and "Death" in Shakespeare's *Romeo and Juliet*

Act / Scene	"Love"	"Death"	Act / Scene	"Love"	"Death"
Act 1, Scene 1	22	4	Act 3, Scene 1	3	3
Act 1, Scene 2	5	0	Act 3, Scene 2	8	6
Act 1, Scene 3	5	0	Act 3, Scene 3	9	12
Act 1, Scene 4	11	1	Act 3, Scene 4	3	0
Act 1, Scene 5	5	0	Act 3, Scene 5	10	5
Act 2, Scene 1	11	1	Act 4, Scene 1	7	6
Act 2, Scene 2	29	2	Act 4, Scene 2	1	0
Act 2, Scene 3	10	1	Act 4, Scene 3	0	1
Act 2, Scene 4	5	0	Act 4, Scene 4	0	0
Act 2, Scene 5	7	1	Act 4, Scene 5	5	10
Act 2, Scene 6	5	1	Act 5, Scene 1	2	2
			Act 5, Scene 2	0	0
			Act 5, Scene 3	9	19

you don't seem impressed with the prompt, right? It might not strike you as very computational or very scientific. So, let's add something else." He clicked on the next slide, which included the original uninspiring question, but now with an addition: *Be sure to use both quantitative data (i.e., from the graph and table) and qualitative data (i.e., textual evidence) in your response.*

Now Tom saw eyebrows raise.

"Check this out," Tom went on as he presented a table of data on the screen. "This table shows the frequencies for the keywords *love* and *death* in every scene in the play." (See Table 6.1.) Each row was labeled with the acts and scenes; each column was labeled for the keywords of interest.

"What you now see is precisely how many times in every scene of the play the words *love* and *death* appeared. This doesn't count for other related words, like *lovely*, or topically related words like *passion*. Just the exact words *love* and *death*. That all make sense?"

Heads nodded.

"Next, I am handing out customized graph paper for a little experiment. You will see on the graph paper that the y-axis is labeled from bottom to top with the numbers 0 to 30. The x-axis is labeled a bit more strangely. Each tick mark represents a scene in the play. Working in small groups, I am asking you to spend the next ten minutes plotting the data from the table for *love* and *death* on your graphs. Use different colors or lines to make it clear in your line graphs which plots are for love and which are for death."

Participants got to work, frequently looking up at the table on the screen as they plotted their data. Tom overheard one participant sigh, saying that scribbling points on a graph is not what reading literature is all about. Tom agreed completely, but said nothing. The real fun hadn't started yet.

After ten minutes, Tom took pictures of a few graphs with his phone, sending them up onto the screen so the whole group could see.

"Whose graph is this one?" Tom asked.

A balding man in a green short-sleeved shirt raised his hand. "It's mine."

"Would you talk us through what you see?"

"Sure. At first, there wasn't much of a surprise really. You can see that in the first two acts of the play the word *love* is used way more often. In the last two acts, the word *death* is used more often."

Tom nodded.

"But as my group kept talking about it, we noticed two things."

"What were they?"

"First, we noticed that in Act 3, Scene 1, the two keywords are used the same number of times. One of my colleagues pointed out that it is in that scene that the conflict of the play really heats up when Tybalt kills Mercutio."

"So what? Why is that interesting?" a voice asked from the back of the room.

Turning behind him, the teacher continued.

"It's interesting because the numerical data drew our attention to a moment in the play that is actually significant from a literary perspective. The numbers aren't random. They show patterns very clearly. So the fact that a simple graph could pull our attention to an important scene surprised us."

Participants began revisiting their own graphs. Some making notes, others erasing marks.

Tom asked, "That's really intriguing. You said you had two points. What was the second?"

"The second observation is in the last scene of the play. That's where everything comes to a tragic end with both Romeo and Juliet killing themselves."

"And what did you see there? I have the same data, same graph even, and I don't notice anything," a woman with brown hair inquired.

"Oh, look at Act 5, Scene 3. The word *love* had really dropped off in frequency throughout the second half of the play. But then, in the last scene the word spikes again. *Death* is used a lot too, but *love* comes out of nowhere. Look at the graph: It's like love is chasing death. That's a pretty profound observation given the prompt we got."

Data

Now, all eyes were on the graph on the screen. Two participants got up to look at the plots more closely. One teacher began tracing the lines on his paper with two fingers to see how the two keywords interrelated.

"So," Tom asked after a couple of minutes, "what questions or insights are coming to mind about the relationship between love and death in the play? Talk with your group briefly and then let's hear what you got."

Participants talked excitedly for three minutes, pointing to the data table, studying the graphs, and even pulling up digital copies of the play on their laptops and phones. After the volume in the room dipped to a hum, Tom reengaged.

"Who would like to start?"

The speaker for one group reported that they wondered exactly how the words *love* and *death* were used in Act 3, Scene 1. Because it was a scene where the two words were used equally and it was a key scene where a main character dies, they wanted to examine more closely exactly how Shakespeare used them.

"We only got to look briefly. But we did notice that the words are not used like they are earlier in the play. Earlier in the play, when the word love is used, it's all rainbows and sunshine and bliss. But when love is used in this scene, it's way more loaded. Look. When Romeo encounters Tybalt early in the scene, he says, 'Tybalt, the reason that I have to love thee / Doth much excuse the appertaining rage / To such a greeting. Villain am I none. / Therefore farewell; I see thou knowest me not.' Romeo's love for Tybalt is confused. It's a forced love because of Tybalt's relationship to Juliet. Romeo loves Juliet so he has to love Tybalt. I think they're cousins or something."

At this point, most participants had pulled up the play and were scrolling through the scenes. Some were using the search feature on web pages to find the words *love* and *death* to see how they were used, then compared them with what they saw on their line graphs. In a matter of a half-hour, that group of teachers had confidently begun to ignore the false separation of science and letters, strutting through the gates with a newfound confidence that computational methods belonged to no single discipline. Certainly not STEM alone. Computationality served only one's curiosity.

Uncovering Subconcepts

Believe it or not, you can learn a great deal about how data operate from the mixed literary analysis assignment described earlier. In what follows, let's unpack a series of subconcepts from the Blueprint and explore ways to weave them into other content areas.

Sensors and Datasets

The Blueprint defines **sensors** and **datasets** by framing their relationship to data. The team writes, "Data is collected by sensors such as video cameras or thermostats, or from other datasets such as government data, or your digital activity. Data from sensors and datasets must always be cleaned, to ensure its accuracy and usability." To clarify, data *can* be collected by sensors, but that's not always the case. Sensors relate to datasets, but are not the same thing. Sensors are used by computers to detect phenomena in the environment and to do something based on that detection. You ever go to a restroom, wash your hands, and wave them under a paper towel dispenser? A little light flashes; paper towel appears. There is a motion sensor beneath the dispenser that detects your hand's movement. The sensor constantly sends out a little signal. When your hand interrupts the signal, it activates the dispenser. It is the same kind of device that makes doors open automatically, vacuums autonomously clean your living room, and hands-free sinks operate. Other sensors can detect things like heat, sound, and even smell.

While there are no sensors used in the mixed literary assignments, two datasets are used. The first dataset is the text of *Romeo and Juliet*. It is a digital text file consisting of Shakespeare's very own words. Like most text data, the play is what we call unstructured data. That means it is not stored in a spreadsheet, but rather it appears in a way that might appeal to humans but is very hard for machines to process easily. The second dataset is the table of word frequencies for *love* and *death*. In that case, the data are presented in a structured manner, with each row representing an act and scene in the play and each column representing a keyword. Then, for each keyword, we see the number of times the word appeared in each act. All neat and tidy.

There are lots of other forms of data that can be used in such activities. For example, you can use methods of analyzing texts to count the number of times specific pronouns or punctuation marks are used. On a more advanced level, you can generate a sentiment score for each sentence or paragraph in a novel. A sentiment score uses an algorithm to estimate whether the words in a text are mostly positive or mostly negative. Marketing companies use such means to track how their brands are talked about on social media. That's just the tip of the iceberg, just some data you can generate for literature.

With the advent of the Internet, there are tons of ways to find interesting datasets. For example, sites like Kaggle or Data World archive data from myriad sources. With just a few clicks, you can find sets of data on a range of topics:

movie reviews from last summer, calorie counts in fast-food chains, voting records of elected officials, test scores for all students in the United States, player statistics for your favorite soccer team, and on and on. By making cultural datasets more accessible, it becomes easier for teachers and students to dabble in the world of data.

Data Abstraction and Storage

In order to create datasets like those used in the mixed literary analysis assignment, it was necessary to **abstract** and **store** data from the original Shakespearean text. Abstraction and storage go hand in hand because, as described in the Blueprint, "data is represented in computers as binary, but humans save and use data on computers as lists, databases, key-value pairs, etc." So how did Tom abstract and store the text of *Romeo and Juliet* for his assignment? In this case, Tom started with an electronic version of the play freely available online. Teams of volunteers for websites like Project Gutenberg already did the painstaking work of transcribing the Bard's tragedy. But still, the transcribed play doesn't give you the word frequencies or anything like that. Creating that simple data table required that Tom abstract and store data.

Tom wrote a rough computer program that automatically broke up the play into scenes, counted every word in every scene, and then stored the tallies in a structured manner called a dataframe. Then all Tom had to do was to save the data in a spreadsheet, and Bob's your uncle! (Or Bill's your bard, whichever you prefer.) It might help to see what this process looks like a bit more closely. Just know that you do not have to program or write code like what you are about to see. It's just for illustration purposes in an effort to better understand abstraction and storage.

First, Tom programs the computer to read a text file that contains the play, which he downloaded from Project Gutenberg. Remember, a text file like that is unstructured data. It's really hard for a computer to do anything with it. So, Tom tells the computer to try to read the text file as a type of dataframe called a tibble. When the computer does so, it creates a rough table in which each row has one whole line from the play until whoever typed it up pressed Enter. The code to achieve this looks like this:

```
rj <- read_lines("/rj.txt")
rj_tb <- as_tibble(rj)
```

It kind of looks silly, doesn't it? Just two little lines does all that. Next, Tom has to tell the computer to take the tibble that he just made and to break it up differently. Specifically, he wants the computer to do three things: identify every line number, break the text up into scenes of the play by automatically detecting the word "Scene" at the beginning of a new line, and then create a new table that gives each individual word its own row, with columns for line numbers and scene numbers.

```
Tidy_rj <- rj_tb %>%
mutate(linenumber = row_number(),
scenes = cumsum(str_detect(value, regex("^Scene",
ignore_case = FALSE)))) %>%
   unnest_tokens(word, value)
```

Now that the text is restructured logically—remember that it was unstructured data up to this point and pretty useless to a machine—Tom needs to know precisely how many times the words *love* and *death* were used. He tells the computer to group the text by scene, count how many times every word in the play is used per scene, and then make a new table with those word counts. Then, all Tom has to do to narrow the table down to *love* and *death* is to filter out every other word.

```
count_rj <- tidy_rj %>%
group_by(scenes) %>%
count(word, sort = TRUE) %>%
ungroup %>%
complete(scenes, word,
         fill = list(n = 0))
love <- filter(count_rj, word == "love")
death <- filter(count_rj, word == "death")
rj_set <- bind_rows(love, death)
```

Finally, after all that, Tom writes a simple line of code to tell the computer to take that new table, which he calls "rj_set," and store it as a good old-fashioned spreadsheet. He types:

```
write_csv(rj_set, "rj-set.csv")
```

Sometimes we might think that data are something that are handed to us, created mysteriously by others in far-away places. What is important to note about this example of code is that you yourself can abstract and store data about virtually anything. And your students can too.

Transformation and Visualization

A table of data might be interesting (or not!), but in order to generate insight, one has to **transform** and **visualize** the data. The Blueprint defines these terms as the computer's ability to "make looking at data easier by allowing us to quickly visualize data in different ways; to break up a big problem into manageable pieces, operate on each piece independently, and then put all the pieces back together." It's true that computers can transform and visualize data rapidly. But humans can do it too, as we saw in the example earlier. In the case of *Romeo and Juliet*, workshop participants had to take the data that were provided and transform them from a table to a graph. The process of visualization then makes it possible to gain insights about the play. Approaching that process without a computer can, in fact, help students and teachers better understand what it is that computers do so swiftly.

There are many benefits to approaching the transformation and visualization process manually. For instance, if students were to count the appearances of words by hand, the tediousness of the exercise carries with it an opportunity to understand the benefits and problems of counting words at all. In counting the appearance of the word *love*, a student might question whether or not to include words like *loving* or *lover* or even *kiss*. In posing those questions, the student gains invaluable critical insight into what computers do so confidently and quickly. In the code where we use the *count* function, does that count variations of words or just the exact words? That question really matters in analyzing literature because it will affect the kinds of insights readers can cull from the visualization. Such questions empower students and teachers to be more digitally discerning, more computationally critical.

Similarly, in manually plotting the line graph, students have to patiently place each point on the graph and in doing so have more time to make connections and pose questions about how the numbers relate to the text. In one workshop, Tom heard a teacher notice aloud while placing a point on the graph that, "Oh, this is where the balcony scene happens!" That iterative process of connecting the quantitative to the qualitative, the fact to the fiction, is a rich part of what English teachers call meaning-making or English professors might call hermeneutics. Again, what appears to be two separate worlds of computers and content-area instruction are often closer than they appear at first.

Feedback Loops and Automation

Feedback loops and **automation** refer strictly to things that computers do while processing data. As per the Blueprint team, "Automation is controlled by data. Some automation uses data from outside the automated system, like time. Other automation uses data on the output of the system, like temperature." But feedback loops and automation also have correlates in the workshop example provided earlier that merit a brief discussion. In the mixed literary analysis workshop example, teachers worked collaboratively to create and make sense of the data. After teachers created their graphs, Tom asked them to first discuss in pairs what they saw: In your graphs, what surprises you and what doesn't? After sharing together, Tom asked couples of teachers to pair up with each other into small groups to pose questions about each other's graphs. Then, Tom asked the small groups to share their insights on a live document on the screen at the front of the room. As all groups shared summaries of their notes, Tom was able to facilitate a whole-group conversation.

What we just described is a systematic feedback loop in which teachers have circumscribed opportunities to hear and provide feedback on a shared task. The word *systematic* is important. It is not uncommon for teachers to ask students to share with a partner or think–pair–share. But in such activities, it is vital that the questions being explored and the quality of the sharing are planned in advance and held accountable in real time in practice. Otherwise, the result can be glib and wan.

 ## In Sum

Data are all around us. Whether they are hidden in the photos we upload to social media sites or abstracted from the lines of great works of literature, data are fundamentally human. It can be tempting to think of data as uniquely digital or as belonging exclusively to content areas most associated with STEM. But to do so ignores the fact that human beings have always recognized and created data around them. What's more, human beings have often relied on stories as ways to convey understanding of data. In Homer, for example, the poet includes lists of names of soldiers and battles and other kinds of historical data. Such catalogs, as they are known, are really kinds of data that have been woven together in narrative form in an effort to ensure future generations will have access to a culture's history.

There is an important lesson there for us. Data do very little good in the world when valued for their own sake. Sophisticated datasets abstracted from the recesses of modern life are only as valuable as the stories they help us tell, the questions they help us pose. Whether you are collecting humidity readings at a local pond or counting keywords in an age-old play, computationality must ultimately serve humanity. Not the humanities, but humanity—a shared human existence. Our classrooms can become places where numbers and letters intermingle in enriching ways, where data are embraced for all their variety and vitality. It is as simple as reimagining what counts.

Connections to Content Areas

Data are everywhere. That includes the major content areas in schools and districts. When teachers begin their learning experiences with data, especially data that students perceive as authentic and culturally responsive, teachers can be confident that the discussions that emerge will be rooted in a kind of concreteness that can be examined and explored *ad infinitum*. Let's look at some brief illustrations.

English Language Arts

In addition to mixed literary analyses, think about the way basic literary analysis operates. When students examine literature, they are often asked to identify specific literary elements and to interpret how the author uses such elements to achieve some kind of effect on readers. The process of identifying literary elements or quotations in a text constitute a process of data abstraction. Students are taking raw unstructured data—the text—and they are abstracting from it discrete data points they can use to formulate a literary argument.

History

Similar to how data might operate in ELA, in history class students are also asked to examine primary source documents in order to identify significant words or parts of the documents as they relate to a particular theme or question. At its core, such identification is a process of historical data abstraction. Further, when students annotate a primary source document, history teachers will be quick to note that they also have to be able to organize all their abstracted information in an orderly way so they can use it in an essay, for example. The process of intentionally organizing abstracted data can be referred to as storage.

Science

Science class has, at its best, embraced the place of data in the curriculum. One classic example consists of students using simple sensors like thermometers to gather data about the natural world. Students might track the temperature of a makeshift greenhouse to determine the effects of cloud cover on plant growth. Groups of students quickly develop datasets that can be transformed and visualized as part of a traditional lab report assignment.

Math

Math teachers will feel quite at home with the idea of using data in their classroom practice. It can be interesting to extend such work by looking at the way data are used in more popular forms of data journalism. For example, websites like *FiveThirtyEight* and *The Pudding* routinely collect large interesting datasets that they transform and visualize into profoundly engaging visual essays. In addition to the essays themselves, teachers will find the technical notes chock full of concepts and explanations about the mathematical decisions underlying the projects.

The Arts

In musical and visual arts, the concept of remix can be useful in exploring the idea of data abstraction. When artists remix another work, they often isolate a specific idea—like a riff from a piece of music or the style of a painting—and then rework it into their own creation. That process of isolating something specific in order to retrieve and reuse it is fundamentally one of data abstraction.

For Further Exploration

- Read | *FiveThirtyEight*, a data science website that covers a range of cultural and political topics: https://fivethirtyeight.com/
- Read | *The Pudding*, a data journalism site that does fascinating projects in which data are used to tell visual stories about society: https://pudding.cool/
- Explore | Kaggle, a repository for tons of datasets that you and your students can explore in a range of academic contexts: https://www.kaggle.com/
- Explore | Project Gutenberg, a collection of e-texts for literature in the public domain: https://www.gutenberg.org/

7 Networks

As the Blueprint team defines it, "Networks, like the Internet, allow computers to interface with other computers through a set of rules, or protocols, that define how computers send and receive data." That's true. But if words like "interface" and "protocols" intimidate you, just think of it in terms of how human beings communicate. Our story of the missing pawn serves as a helpful case in point.

Weeks passed as Tom waited for the missing pawn to arrive. Weeks, plural. During that time, Tom tried to leverage different communication strategies to get things resolved more quickly. At first, the chessboard company told him to send an email to their support team, who would resolve the issue. He did, sharing his story, his heartbreak, and verifying his order information. They sent the pawn in the mail, not rushed or express. Just sent it in the mail with the urgency of a balloon released on a windless day. Two weeks passed. No pawn. When Tom asked the company where his pawn was, they responded that it had arrived. They were right. The pawn did arrive, at the wrong address.

Over social media, Tom asked how on earth it was possible to ship the chessboard to the right address only to send the missing pawn to the wrong address. Clearly the company was using two different systems for shipment and for support. What became evident over time was that the people who packed the order were different from the people monitoring the company's social media, and they were all different from the people who were responsible for responding to support requests. In our globalized world, they were likely thousands of miles apart from each other.

Human communication is itself complex. Anyone who has ever been in a relationship knows so. Sometimes it is challenging enough to communicate even simple things to the ones you love. Sometimes it helps to have strategies for speaking to each other, especially when the topic could be a sensitive one. As a father, Tom has had to learn to mind his tone of voice when speaking with his son. It comes across as angry and judgmental when he doesn't mean it to be. When you add asynchronous written language to the equation, communication gets even harder. Look at the kinds of unproductive and heated conversations that can happen over email chains, texts, and in online discussions. The simple act of communicating can be unfathomably challenging. That's true for personal communications, professional communications, and computational communications. So as we begin to discuss what is meant by networks and how one might explore them in one's classroom, just remember that for all its computationality, the challenges of communication networks are very human and very known to you already.

(As for the pawn, it ultimately arrived fourteen days after it was reported missing. Tom was alone in his apartment when it came, which might have been for the best. Tom set up the board, connected it to his phone, and began. He played his first game against the computer on a novice level and lost. It was an anticlimactic inaugural game, the Dionysian ecstasy that started the whole thing bedimmed.)

Waves of Light Through the Darkness

"Come what come may, time and the hour run through the roughest day."
—*Macbeth* I.iii

Anyone who knows Pam knows how important light is in her life. It energizes her and fills her soul. Her favorite season is springtime, daybreak is her favorite time of day, and she will affectionately tell you that by 9:00 a.m. half the day is over. How could anyone possibly sleep in until midday? In early 2007, her instructional team leader let her know to pack up her teaching materials because she would be moving out of her portable classroom up to the second floor to Room A211. She was relocating to the penthouse! Squealing with joy, her response was, "I love that classroom! I love the way the light comes in early in the morning." Her team leader got a kick out of her response, but Pam believed it was just her inner Transcendentalist breaking out. Whether it was teaching Miller, Emerson, Thoreau, or Shakespeare, the light of knowledge always burns bright in A211. So did the light of the sun.

Each new school year brought excitement and a wonderful feeling of new ideas to enrich the lives of the students who walked into Pam's classroom. It was now fall. Outside, the air was crisp and the feeling of autumn had broken through Georgia's oppressive summer heat. Its grasp had finally released its encumbrance over all living things. It should have been a time to bask in the freshness of how things are supposed to change with the beginning of every new school year. Except, it was already ten weeks into the semester and a feeling of desperation crept over Pam as she stood at the front of her classroom looking at thirty-two apathetic seniors engaged in some trending story on Instagram about Kim Kardashian's derriere.

Pam briefly drifted off into a distant memory of a conversation she was having with her long-time English teaching colleague, who was now a freshly minted assistant principal and her evaluator. Earlier that year, she stopped by Pam's room to ask her how she felt about teaching seniors. She went on enthusiastically to tell her that Pam would be the ideal fit to teach British literature.

In her effervescent voice and ear-to-ear grin, Pam remembers her supervisor saying, "We think you have an excellent rapport with your students. We need you and think you would make great connections with our senior co-taught kids."

A wave of darkness descended upon Pam as the reality set in. She quickly understood the challenges of being "voluntold" and tried to appear happy about gaining the responsibility of two new preps. This would require her to spend her summer learning a great deal more content.

At first she thought, "There goes my summer."

Pam was unsure what she had done to deserve this punishment. She was confident in her pedagogy and previously relished in the delight that comes with being a ten-year veteran American literature teacher. A delight that was imbued with the familiarity of knowing the texts verbatim and being able to rely on having already created dozens of creative, engaging lessons. Lessons purposely designed with her extensive knowledge of American literature and familiarity with the areas of New England often described in the curriculum.

Pam was in her teacher comfort zone, so she thought—or was it complacency merely masked by comfort?

The end of the school year was a blur. Summer vacation blazed through like a lightning bolt, and eventually the fresh October winds blew in. Waves of light poured into her classroom as Pam returned to the reality of students still hyperfocused on their phone screens. And then the distortions set in.

Distortions in Learning

During those first weeks of the semester, Pam realized that traditional teaching methods were no longer making connections with her students. In the not-so-distant past, lecture and direct instruction provided a familiar and time-tested approach to skills-based summative assessments.

She realized that fewer and fewer students engaged in recreational reading and writing for pleasure. Even though Pam thought the students were engaged, they craved more: more creative writing, more interactivity, more collaboration, more electronic access, and more technology-based lessons. Her students were unapologetic about their obsession with their electronic devices, and this conflicted with Pam's direct instructional pedagogy. She was up for the challenge because she loves technology and futurism. Her students were primed and ready for a new challenge. This challenge was timely because the landscape of education was rapidly changing.

Pam took a reflective approach to her teaching style and concluded that her pedagogy should undergo a transformation to better meet the needs of the students. A new day had dawned and the light of change was on the horizon. So began a refreshed approach towards providing a collaborative, high-tech, and engaging learning environment.

October slid into November and the *Macbeth* unit quickly appeared on the horizon. In Act I, Pam used two research-based teaching methods. She focused on building student knowledge of archaic language through a gallery walk exercise and student-led intimate discussion circles with preselected groups. In Act II, students completed a film analysis of the Baz Luhrman version of *Macbeth* where they identified direct and indirect characterization. In addition, they were responsible for an in-depth study of how the characters used language as a function of emotion. In Act III, students were taught theatrical elements and how to "block" a scene. The skills they learned during the instruction of each act provided fertile ground for students to scaffold into the skills they needed to have success in Act V. Pam knew that if she didn't find something innovative quickly for Act V, her students would run out of stamina to finish the play. They would disengage altogether. Change had to happen soon.

Seeing Through the Lens of Change

Pam has always had a devout passion for learning new technologies. For decades, she had been driven to combine science with the study of the English language. In 2005, she presented a poster in a symposium at the University of Georgia College of Education on *Incorporating the Discourse of Nanotechnology into English Education Communities*. At the time, not many people knew what nanotechnology was, much less the impact it would have on society in the future. Her fascination with the study of language and its connection to science and technology was an area of focus that she felt needed to be addressed. Her capacity to think outside the box and make connections to abstract ideas has served her well as an educator. It was this same type of focus that led her to seek out a nontraditional way of having her students learn Act V of *Macbeth*.

As mentioned earlier, it became painfully apparent that even after several high-interest teaching strategies were employed in class, her students were still losing their stamina and interest in *Macbeth*. This presented a problem, and Pam was determined to find or create a learning experience that resonated with her students, yet had the rigor necessary to meet the county standards in English language arts (ELA). She researched ideas on how to approach her final segment of teaching *Macbeth*.

Pam sought out and discovered an interesting learning concept from two professors in Manhattan. Tom and Gerald, the co-authors of this book, created a project for their university teaching cohort where they had students write code and build a robot that would act out scenes in a play. They produced a project called BardBots where their students programmed robots to perform scenes in Shakespeare's plays.

Pam decided to modify Tom and Gerald's project and asked her students to have robots act out a scene from *Macbeth* and emote as though they were human. In and of itself, the idea is unique, and programming robots to act as humans was one way of creating an awareness in her students to be cognizant of what is happening in the world around them. The exercises they completed required collaboration with each other to achieve the specified outcome of the project. They had to work and communicate with each other to fulfill the requirements. A secondary learning goal for this exercise was designed with the intent that students would develop a wider understanding of how language has power, for human beings and for computers.

Under the auspices of Babble Lab, a center for digital humanities pedagogy and research Tom co-founded with English professor Dr. Kelley Kreitz, Tom and Gerald's BardBots project offered a complete unit plan that Pam studied to see if it would be feasible to duplicate with her students, and many logistical questions arose. Five key issues would have to be resolved if Pam was to facilitate the BardBots project:

1. Can relevant learning targets be extracted from this project?
2. Will the lessons presented improve higher-level thinking skills?
3. How will this project reinforce student literacy and meet literacy goals?
4. Can the instructional methods used be reinforced with research-based learning strategies?
5. How will the activities be formally and summatively assessed?
6. Are there robots available that do not have to be purchased?

So many questions needed concrete answers before Pam could proceed. Issues were still in limbo. Yet she blazed down the trail of tackling a new challenge simultaneously teaching both computer coding and Act V of *Macbeth*.

Pam diligently worked through what she wanted to accomplish by the end of the project. First and foremost, she would have to be sure that students understood the interpersonal dynamics between the characters in Act V. She wanted them to be able to duplicate the emotional constructs that humans embody when acting. Her expectations were for the students to replicate these actions with the robots. (Tom and Gerald used mBots for BardBots. Pam used a comparable inexpensive robot called Finch robots.) A clear picture was beginning to develop. After informally surveying the students, they showed great interest in writing code to have robots perform. Initially, she was concerned about whether the students would read Act V at all. They were visibly becoming fatigued with the language and continuing forward to finish the play. Yet BardBots required a pedagogy focused on having students collaborate, move around the room, and help each other to learn how to write basic computer code.

But for Pam, the idea of integrating computer science into her ELA classroom had the effect of pulling a curtain open. There was something illuminating about it. And you know how Pam feels about light.

Seeing the Light

The grip of helplessness released its ugly hold on how Pam would approach the remainder of the semester. She found herself enlightened and energized as she thought of ways she could intertwine the study of the English language with the study of computer languages. It occurred to her how similar constructs are used when students draft an essay and when a developer writes and debugs code.

At the end of a long weekend of research, Pam listed all of the tasks she needed to complete before she would approach her administrator and request permission to start introducing her own version of BardBots, which she called Macbot. She emailed the AP Computer Science teacher Chris Michael and explained what she was trying to accomplish with her Macbot concept. He was intrigued. After they discussed her idea, Chris loaned her thirteen Finch robots. At that moment, Pam realized that selecting the identical robot from the BardBot project was less important than the goal of integrating computational thinking into her pedagogy as part of her plan to remix her curriculum in order to problem-solve and work through challenges that help students develop sharp critical thinking skills. Together, they loaded the necessary integrated development environment onto her teacher laptop. Students would need to use Snap! code to run the Finch robots. Because the Snap! environment uses graphical, colored, interlocking coding blocks (much like Scratch mentioned previously), the language is easy to learn and uses self-explanatory terms students use to make the Finch robots fulfil the commands they chose to act out their assigned scenes.

Pam made an appointment to share her ideas in detail with her supervisor and what she was she was planning to teach each day for the next two weeks. Having explained her purpose, identifying research-based teaching methods and the standards she would cover, she understood that her administrator may shoot down her idea at any stage during their meeting. Hoping that her idea would pique the administrator's interest, Pam took great care to explain the outcomes she expected from her classroom "experiment." The following day, Pam received an email from the administrator stating how excited she was and couldn't wait to see the robots in action.

Be the "Guide on the Side Instead of the Sage on the Stage"

As she began the project, Pam recalled how during grad school her professor Dr. Tom Hébert enthusiastically stated, "Remember when working with your students, always be the Guide on the Side, instead of the Sage on the Stage. Carefully consider that your students may not be as interested as you are in your lesson." His words have frequently reverberated in Pam's mind throughout the course of the project. She intentionally planned for her students to move around as much as possible to work together solving the various problems that arose within their individual groups.

On the first day, Pam had her twelfth-grade students in British literature get into groups that she created. She appointed a group leader. Each group self-selected who would "perform" which character in the assigned scene in Act V. She empowered students to make these decisions among themselves in order to create a sense of "team" within each group. Pam recalls that students were very excited to see who was in their group. She also asked them to volunteer if they had experience with computer programming or coding.

Prior to beginning this lesson, it was essential to think through all aspects of the project. Having small groups of three students, all members in each group were tasked with responsibilities for which they were best suited. The team leader was selected from students who had a fairly good computational aptitude or who were taking one of the CS courses at the school. Having these students as team "anchors" helped tremendously because they could troubleshoot and assist other students who had difficulty with their projects.

Seven students volunteered to be group leaders. In a quick meeting before the project started, Pam explained how the group leaders would take on a leadership role in one of the seven newly formed groups. They were tasked with heading up their own teams and an additional support role to provide guidance to other groups that might struggle with the technical portions of the assignment. By empowering her students to make their own decisions, they were able to solve problems that came about as a result of their struggles with learning how to write code in the robots' programming language called Snap!.

Students used the Folger Shakespeare Library edition of *Macbeth*'s Act V to create an annotated Prompt Book. Together, they decided what functions they wanted their robot to complete and how they would have it "perform" as their character of choice. Pam employed a gradual release of responsibility by allowing students to take ownership of how they were going to present their understanding of literary and dramatic techniques in coordination with their demonstration of plot dynamics. She gave students a rubric that outlined her expectations for the robot performance activities.

Students had already completed a Prompt Book activity for their human performance of Act III, which made them familiar with "blocking" out stage placement and location. Her students were experienced and understood the expectations of completing this exercise—only this time with an added robotic twist.

The Macbot Project in Action

Once assigned to their teams, some students resisted the idea of what Pam was asking them to do. Like any project, some chose not to participate and some did the minimum. This created a weak spot in their human network. Eventually, they realized that this project was not one that had been completed before and joined in with their team members to complete their assigned responsibilities.

Many students became frustrated because they had developed clear objectives and the processes they wanted their robots to complete, but had difficulty getting the program to execute their desired outcome. They had to write and rewrite their code to get the robots to do what they intended. Pam recalls how students were particularly challenged with programming the Finch robots to blink their noses a certain color to represent an emotion that the character in *Macbeth* would have displayed in their scene. By process of elimination with the placement of the "blink" block, one student discovered how to get the Finch robot to blink its beak a color that is symbolic of the emotion that character might be feeling at that point in the scene. It was no coincidence that the Lady Macbeth Finch robot blinked her "nose" red as she read her infamous soliloquy. Another group programmed their Finch robots to hold solid green and blue "noses" to symbolize the colors of their clan as they marched into battle in Act V.4. For instance, when one team discovered how to configure the blocks in a specific order to complete an action, Pam asked them to reach out to the struggling groups. They assisted the other teams with a solution and recommended code to use as a workaround solution.

As the students proceeded with their planning during the design phase, they developed goals for their robot performance and by methodically working through their objectives, they drafted, revised, added, and eliminated the steps that their Macbot would perform. They modeled the desired actions they wanted robots to perform and tested them out in the Snap! Sandbox (see Figure 7.1). Pam required students to have their robots "speak" the dialogue of their individual character. Soon, they discovered the flexibility to make the Finch robots "speak," but there was no inflection. The code did have its limitations. The characters spoke in a computerized voice that was monotonous and showed no emotion. One group was not satisfied with the lack of emotion in the computer voice. Another group discovered a workaround solution by recording their lines into Voice Notes on their phones and then

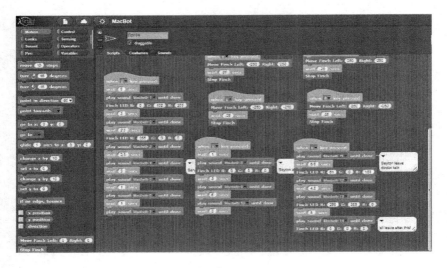

Figure 7.1 Macbot movements in Snap! code.

played them while performing the scene. Pam recalls how gratifying it was to see each one of her students participating in revolutionizing the curriculum.

For several class periods, Pam provided direct instruction to show the characteristics and actions each colored block represents. This provided the skills for each team to write the code necessary to have their Finch robots perform actions that executed the movements they desired. They had fun building their program code and testing out their actions in the Snap! sandbox. Each group made progress through trial and error. They discovered that Snap! code was easy to use because of the instinctive nature of the color-coded command blocks. (See more about block-based coding in Chapters 3 and 5.)

For some students who had advanced knowledge of coding, they found it easier to write text-based code in the compiler.

In both situations, Pam explained to students that languages all require a specific syntax to "work" correctly. She went on to explain how a program will not run if the code is not written or developed properly. The syntax and commands must be in the proper order for the code to execute. During one class, Pam projected an example of a poorly written paragraph with incorrect punctuation and grammar on the interactive white board. She then projected the Snap! application on next to the hand written text to show the similarities between the two languages and what each communicated to the reader. She also reminded students how their programs did not work when the improper code was used, much like when writing an essay and using improper grammar and sentence structure. They understood how the similarities were surprisingly alike. The parallels between drafting an essay and writing computer code became apparent to all. Students experienced how both written English and Snap! code paralleled one another. This revelation indicated how incredibly alike both forms of language network to translate into communication. A communication that may either be translated in a wired or wireless form.

Each robot connected to an individual laptop via USB cable. This presented somewhat of a challenge and required students to carry their laptops as their robots performed their scene. The goal of the exercise was to have the Finch robots maneuver across the "stage" as though they were actors. As students became familiar with Snap!, they quickly realized that some of their performance ideas would require multiple robots to complete a specific task to play out the scene, but it was too time and labor intensive. After this realization, they modified their code to meet the limitations of their robots—just like authors who revise based on readers' feedback.

During students' cold read of Act V, they were instructed to analyze and integrate the key lines and dramatic techniques into the essence of their robot's performance. This activity was a progressive task that involved annotating the Prompt

Book and modifying the robot's behavior to function within the limitations of the technology available. At the beginning, Pam was concerned that students would get bored with the play. With the inception of integrating technology into her ELA class, the students never complained that they were reading Act V multiple times so that they could achieve the objectives outlined in the assignment. Excellent group dialogue was present as students made executive decisions, which affected the potential outcome of their performances. The blending and integration of technology took hold.

Students constructed their own internal schemas, which allowed them to scaffold their understanding of how they would allow their bots to act as they planned during their blocking activities. During one class period, they planned out how they would write the Snap! code to get their robots to perform the necessary actions required for the project. Silently, Pam feared the worst. She often thought, "What if this project is a disaster?" At the end of each class period, she required her students to post their thoughts in her class discussion board so she could get an idea of how they were feeling about the progress of their groups. In addition, she required them to read journal articles that discussed why it is important to integrate CS principles into other core subjects. Their reflections on these readings documented their understanding of both the content of Act V and the higher-level purpose of the Macbot project. By requiring cross-discussion posts, students were able to network with each other to validate their ideas in relation to their daily activities.

At the conclusion of the two weeks, each group presented their rendition of their assigned scene in front of a "mock stage" painted by one of the students. They presented Act V chronologically, and many had technological difficulties. Every challenge represented the strengths and weaknesses of the internal network they had built within their group and among their peers. If one aspect of the "network" was down, the project faltered and students had to reconfigure a solution to the problems that arose when running their Snap! code. Group members relied on each other to work through their difficulties. As Pam watched students' Macbot performances, she experienced the warmth of a radiant light. Not the sun's rays from without, but the light of pedagogical innovation bursting out from within.

Uncovering Subconcepts

In her pedagogy, Pam had set out to try a dramatically new teaching strategy. One that was innovative, creative, and rigorous enough to challenge her students, yet provide high interest. Pam's story also helps us begin to understand subconcepts related to networks. Recall that one's understanding of human networks helps demystify computational networks.

Trust

Trust is implicit when you are an educator. Administrators, parents, stakeholders, and, most importantly, students place formidable trust in the role teachers impart in providing knowledge to future generations. All of them rely on Pam's expertise as an educator. The trust is reciprocated, and she wholeheartedly respects the power that educators have in the classroom. She has tremendous respect for her position and the trust her students have for her. Pam establishes excellent relationships with her students early on in the year and knows when a student trusts and respects her. After earning that trust and respect, students are open to learning new concepts and will happily engage in active classroom activities.

In the world of computationality, **trust** is not dissimilar. The Blueprint writes, "The common thread behind issues of security, privacy and consent is trust. Whenever we connect to a network, we decide our level of trust, based on our security and privacy needs. We implement and monitor protocols to protect those needs." Pam's school had a networking infrastructure that ensured issues of security, privacy, and consent were respected. So do many schools. That's why students sign on to computers with their own unique usernames. It's why administrators can never see a student's password, only help them change it. It's why devices like Finch robots need to be purchased with data security and privacy in mind. Because children will be using them in a safe and secure space.

Protocols

Languages are an integral part of cultural diversity, freedom of expression, and universal access to information and knowledge. The English language is one of the most challenging languages to learn, yet over 1.3 billion people communicate in some form of English. The communication of data and the transfer of information from teacher to student and student to student function within a set of protocols. When the transfer of information is uninterrupted, then the flow of data is smooth and uncorrupted. Processes can be completed, packets can be sent, instructions will be followed or carried out according to the functions indicated in the syntax. Send, synchronize, share, report, and recover.

The Blueprint defines **protocols** thus: "In order to send data from one device to another, the devices must be synchronized, share a syntax for the data, share a method of encryption, and have a way to report and recover from errors." The clearest place to see protocols at work in the Macbot project is when students were trying to pair their robots with the computers. Gerald and Tom agree: It's nearly always a challenge at first. That's because a very narrow protocol is being used to let the computer communicate with the robot. Lots of syntax and encryption issues for both devices to sort out. It might be worth noting, however, that in Pam's language arts class communication was no different. Sending instructions to students indicated a desired function would result in a specific outcome. When Pam's students understood her expectations, things went very smoothly. In fact, if there were no expectations or if her expectations were unclear, then the learning environment in her class would have never had success with the Macbot project.

Physical Internet

Part of what made the Macbot project successful was the technology available to the students and teachers. The school where this project was taught is in a suburb of Metro Atlanta and had recently undergone a retrofit with upgraded routers and bandwidth very capable of handling multiple users on the Wi-Fi at any given time. Also, the school is connected to an extremely fast fiber optic connection that rarely, if ever, experienced slow traffic or lag. Students in Pam's class never experienced difficulty with being able to connect to the network, and as a matter of fact, they took for granted that the technology was available for them to complete the project. This allowed them to be focused on presenting their work to the class instead of dealing with technology failures.

As the Blueprint defines the **physical Internet**, "It is critical to understand the infrastructure of the Internet, including the hardware, companies, governing bodies, etc. that connect your computer to Internet exchanges—where massive networks cross-connect to the undersea fiber-optic cables that connect the world (not satellites)." In our experience, that is something many educators and people have a hard time understanding. For all the appearance of wirelessness, the Internet is only possible with a lot of wires and metal and plastic. Just as the physicality of robots is a helpful reminder to students that the digital and physical worlds are not so separate, so, too, does the ubiquity of cables hiding in the ceilings, access points hanging from the walls, and the very devices themselves remind us that the digital world is hardly as ephemeral as it appears.

Markup

Recall for a moment that part of the intent of Pam's project was to have students examine the code and compare it to how the English language is similar. Pam wanted her students to discover and analyze how language commands structure, sequential functions, and proper syntax. For instance, the inverted syntax in *Macbeth* is difficult and presents a challenge for most people. Disseminating the structure and the archaic language of each line in the play takes patience and concentration to comprehend, synthesize, and deconstruct in order to make sense of what Shakespeare is attempting to convey. While some readers see beautiful language, others see an arduously difficult text to understand.

These English language grammar and syntax rules exist for a reason—to get the language to function the way it was intended. If the syntax or grammar is ill placed or incorrectly used, the intended meaning will be lost in translation. Without grammar rules, language would be subject to any type of interpretation and would result in a great deal of confusion.

There is no difference when writing code to make an app, a program, or a website perform its intended function. **Markup** is a perfect example, which the Blueprint team defines as, "Hypertext Markup Language (HTML) is the standard way to publish information or applications on the Internet. It is a standard agreed upon by the Internet Engineering Task Force (IETF). It is not a programming language, as it doesn't use logic." Without a "standard way" to make information available online, there simply wouldn't be the digital revolution we are experiencing today. It would be informational chaos, a dilapidated digital tower of Babel.

 ## In Sum

In this chapter, Pam's objective was to bring you into her classroom where she took the least likely subject, English, and shone the light on an entirely nontraditional way of getting students to take Shakespeare seriously, integrating computer science principles into daily instruction.

As much as Tom struggled with the lack of communication between two departments that resulted in a missing pawn, he relied on a trusted framework that had provided a system that he had come to rely on to produce and deliver a product he expected. Educators should not remain complacent with historical and even current practice: remember that teaching is a dynamic profession that demands the creation of people who will become productive citizens in society.

Networks

The networking concepts discussed in this chapter began with building trust among students. Good communication results in exciting new challenges for students who will learn vital communication skills that are essential for a collaboration based future. Good communication networks are also the heart and soul of what makes the digital world work at all. The more we understand that idea in our daily lives, the clearer we will be able to see when those communication networks are vulnerable, manipulated, and corrupted. But it starts with knowing what they are in the first place. And who better to show us such things than a 400-year-old playwright? No one, Pam suspects.

 ## Connections to Content Areas

Much like Pam and her experience with the Macbot project, the networking concepts can be employed in other subject areas. This chapter has primarily addressed the integration of computer science principles into ELA at the high school level. Listed here are some conceptual ideas that deal with networks that are primed for further exploration and creative development.

English Language Arts

An oft-taught topic in ELA classrooms is how authors develop characters. One of the key ways this is done is by exploring direct and indirect forms of characterization. In order to unpack indirect characterization, readers have to tune into the way other characters or the narrator encrypts information. A narrator might imply something about a character or use a specific word that is less than appealing to describe a character. Such authorial moves are subtle protocols authors employ as a way to build complex characters—it's about how trustful readers are of narrators, characters, and authors.

History

In history class, teachers often examine the way politics unfold on a micro and macro scale. When it comes to matters of politics and diplomacy, trust is front and center. What are the ways in which trust factored into U.S. foreign policy, for instance? Or, perhaps more darkly, how have espionage and secret codes attempted

121

to control the types of information and disinformation shared across governments throughout history? Fast forwarding to the present, it would be quite understandable to examine current debates about election hacking and the use of social media to spread disinformation. Trust—and what it means for human beings and for computers—has never been a more pressing issue.

Math

Protocols are also really helpful to consider in math classes. This is especially the case when we think about the protocols students use to solve problems, how they show their work to their teachers so that their thinking is clear. There are better and worse ways for students not only to approach solving a problem but to communicate their thought process to their teachers. As many schools move away from overvaluing single correct answers in favor of understanding students' process of solving problems—their thinking—it can be invaluable to invoke the computational idea of protocol.

Science

The human correlates to computational networks are all around us in the natural world. Our bodies are composed of networks, like those neural networks in our brains. What's more, it's not uncommon to map the ways different species or chemicals relate to each other via sophisticated networking maps. It can be quite powerful to make clear to students just how this very natural tendency toward networks is also fundamental to the often-invisible world of the Internet they know so well.

The Arts

Put on your favorite blues or jazz instrumental album. Listen for the protocols at play. It is not uncommon to hear, for instance, a kind of call-and-response practice throughout songs. For example, when a jazz musician takes a solo—say a trumpeter—you might hear the drummer subtly echoing the impromptu rhythm of the soloist, or you might hear the pianist playing a variation of a musical phrasing in the trumpeter's solo. This is all part of jazz protocol: mutually understood ways of communicating music together.

For Further Exploration

- Read | BardBots Project: http://www.babblelab.org/bardbots
- Check out | Birdbrain Technologies: https://www.birdbraintechnologies.com/finch/
- Watch | "The Internet: Packets, Routing & Reliability" by Code.org: https://youtu.be/AYdF7b3nMto
- Watch | "How Computers Work: What Makes a Computer, a Computer?" by Code.org: https://youtu.be/mCq8-xTH7jA
- Read | Lynch, T. L. (2019). Electrical evocations: Computer science, the teaching of literature, and the future of English education. *English Education*, 52(1), 15–37.

8 Getting Started

Over the previous chapters, we have made the case for why computationality should be embedded into all grades and content areas in K–12 settings. We argued that computationality is vital for the future of society, both civically and economically. Then, we offered a brief overview of some of the popular frameworks schools and districts are using as they try to figure out what "computer science for all" means in their communities. Paradoxically, we said that the words *computer* and *science* do more to limit access to computationality than one would think, causing us to say that advocates for robust computer science education in K–12 schools should stop talking so much about computers and the sciences. It was with this in mind that we suggested schools and districts think about how to embed computationality everywhere rather than adding computer science somewhere. New York City's Blueprint for K–12 Computer Science Education is, in our view, the best framework for beginning to do so. Others have their merits, but they are often too specifically geared to narrow computer science classes, or they are too generally presented without the conceptual nuances and clear practical implications that would make them most valuable to schools. It was the Blueprint that gave us the framework needed to organize those middle chapters you just completed, each devoted to a high-level computational concept and its associated subconcepts.

So, now what?

We didn't write this book to be an academic exercise. We wrote it to be useful, which heretofore has taken the shape of real-world illustrations, stories, and ideas for classroom practice. But you don't want to do this work scattershot. You want to be systematic and intentional about it, right? We want you to be, for sure. It is only when you approach this work systematically in your curriculum and instruction that you can be sure computationality is equitably and sustainably available to all children. In what follows, we want to offer a basic step-by-step plan for how to get things off the ground in a way that allows you to be nimble, strategic, and sustainable in making computationality a part of your classroom, school, and district. Here are the main phases for getting started that we suggest:

1. **Huddle**. Form a working group of stakeholders who are committed to learning about computationality, connecting it to your curricular and instructional vision, piloting prototypes, and leading implementation teams over time.
2. **Explore**. Set a time frame within which the working group will review materials about computationality, exchange ideas, and generate insights that will help guide the work moving forward.
3. **Connect**. Review existing curricular and instructional materials—especially things like curriculum maps, achievement data, and planning templates—and for each document, ask yourselves how computationality can deepen and expand the work as it already exists.
4. **Pilot**. Working in vertical or horizontal teams, identify specific assignments that can be designed and piloted in the next one to two months. These might be totally new assignments inspired by some of the examples in this book. Or they might be strategic modifications to existing assignments. Importantly, you want the assessment mechanism for the assignment to explicitly account for the relevant language in the Blueprint.
5. **Evaluate**. Using internal evaluation frameworks already familiar to the school community (i.e., the Danielson Framework, Webb's Depth of Knowledge), evaluate what worked and what didn't work about the pilot. Make adjustments accordingly.
6. **Expand**. Working group leaders divide up and begin meeting with grade- and/or content-level colleagues and teams to share the progress, ideate ways to expand the use of computationality, and set measurable goals for the next three to six months.

In what follows, we will unpack each of these six steps individually. Each section will be anchored in a planning instrument that provides clarity of the contours of the stage in question. As a rule, we honor the fact that every classroom, school, and district is unique. Doubtless, you will want and need to make alterations. However, we will also point out why we designed the instruments the way we did so that any adjustments you make can be done knowingly. Let's get into it.

Getting Started

 # Phase 1: Huddle

Whether you are an individual teacher, a school principal, or a district official, the first phase ensures that you will not walk this path alone. We've broken down the phase into six steps. But before we look at the steps, we warn you that we are going to emphasize the importance of starting with a little word that has big impact: why. In his book *Start with Why: How Great Leaders Inspire Everyone to Take Action*, business professor Simon Sinek argues that when you look at the most effective leaders in recent times, they all have one thing in common. They lead their organizations by focusing on the following: 1) why we do this work, 2) how we do this work, and 3) what we do. That order—why, how, what—can be of immense value to the way educational organizations operate as well. We suspect some readers might be skeptical as we begin referring to business theory in a K–12 education book. But hear us out.

In education, it is our experience that teachers and school leaders are often forced to work in the reverse order. First, they focus on what to teach: a set of tested standards. Second, they focus on how to teach: a teacher-effectiveness framework. Third, they might focus on why they teach what they teach by exploring enduring understandings, big ideas, and other similar why-like aspects of pedagogy. The result of putting the why last is that schools tend to find themselves in reaction or compliance mode. Our days start with that sense of having to check a box rather than with the higher purpose that makes us commit to education in the first place. If someone was to ask you why you get out of bed in the morning, your answer might be something like "because I have to" instead of "because I'm preparing young people to contribute civically and economically to society." But when we start with why, we increase the likelihood that our energy and effort will be guided by what really matters. With that in mind, let's see those six steps.

Step 1.1: Build a Team

Who is on the team? When you involve others in your interests and thinking, you not only get the benefit of their perspective but you also increase the level of personal accountability. It's a lot harder to abandon a project when you have publicly engaged others in its pursuit. Avoid the temptation to go it alone.

Step 1.2: Know Why Everyone is There

Why them? Educators are asked to be in meetings all the time, too often without a clear understanding of why them. State explicitly why each person was invited into the huddle. It could be because they are comfortable with technology, sure. But it can also be because they are skeptical about new initiatives. It could be that they are a creative thinker or a born task-master. Whatever the reasons, be sure to discuss those reasons from the start. It honors everyone's presence in a way that will strengthen the group's work.

Step 1.3: Put Why First

If a parent asked why you—as a teacher, leader, school—educate children, what would your answer be? Remember that there is a lot about the way education is currently framed that makes asking and answering that question really hard. Emphasis is often placed on tests, standards, achievement scores, and teaching measures. Regardless of whether you think such things are good or not, recall that those are *hows* and *whats*—not *whys*. If you want to maximize the work's chances of success, you have to put the why first. Fortunately, most schools and districts have materials that can help. Revisit documents like vision and mission statements. Check out your state's constitution where it articulates why you have a compulsory education system. Look at your curriculum maps and reflect on those big ideas, guiding questions, and enduring understandings that frame learning and teaching.

Step 1.4: Embrace Skepticism

We find it helpful to begin this kind of work—especially when it involves popular technologies—by first assuming that it is a complete waste of time and resources. Be skeptical. Don't start with the assumption that computer science or computational thinking or computationality is necessarily worth focusing on. Assume the opposite. Honor skepticism and dissent. If no one on the team feels that way, play devil's advocate. What would a technophobe at the table say? Or ask the question: What else could we do with our limited time and resources if we abandoned this computationality work right now? Have that conversation. It's real.

Step 1.5: Why Computationality, with Adults

You will have more time to dig into the question of why in Phase 2. Still, now is the time to articulate your short-form understanding. Based on the values of your school district and community, the curiosity and creativity of your students and teachers, and the ideas shared in the previous chapters, why might computer science be worth exploring further in your classroom, school, and district? Really wordsmith a collective response to that question in no more than one or two sentences.

Step 1.6: Why Computationality, with Students

With Step 5 in mind, now shift perspectives. Picture a student raising her or his hand, looking you in the eye, and asking this question: Why are we doing computational stuff in this class? Write a one- to two-sentence response that doesn't evoke tests, college, or because you said so. If time permits, even picture different actual students you have taught who might ask that question in different ways. Again, construct a collective response and wordsmith accordingly.

Once you have had a chance to work through these six steps of Phase 1, it's time to turn your attention to Phase 2: Explore. As you will see, the diligence with which you attended to Phase 1 will directly affect the quality of Phase 2. So double-check your responses in Phase 1, and when you're ready, let's move ahead.

Phase 1: Huddle | Planning Guide

Date: _____   School/District: _____

1. Who is on the team?	2. Why them?

Getting Started

3. If a parent asked you why you—as a teacher, leader, school—educate children, what is your answer? You might review the district's mission statement or vision statement or similar documents, if helpful. Or look at a sample curriculum and see what big ideas drive it.

4. What might a skeptic say about efforts to bring computer science to K–12 schools?	5. Based on what you have read in the previous chapters, why might computer science be worth exploring further in your classroom, school, and district?

6. Picture a student raising her or his hand, looking you in the eye, and asking this question: Why are we doing computational stuff in this class? Write a one- to two-sentence response that doesn't evoke tests, college, or because you said so.

 Fantastic work! You should now have a more concrete understanding of WHY computationality is worth exploring in your community. That move alone will be invaluable. You are ready to roll up your sleeves. Let's move forward to Phase 2: Explore.

Phase 2: Explore

It will not surprise you to hear that when it comes to K–12 computer science education, there is no shortage of ideas and resources floating out there. To be clear, we think there is great potential in those ideas and resources. However, we also think that whether or not that potential is realized has everything to do with how thoroughly your team understands why the work is important, as well as a sense of the strengths and weaknesses of your current organizational structure and culture. We have argued in this book that the key to equitable and sustainable access to K–12 computer science can only really be achieved when it is embedded into the current curriculum in schools, which can be done by emphasizing computationality and computational methods rather than computer science. It is through that lens that we suggest four basic steps to explore what other practices are out there in the world. But remember: some of the practices might slide right into current instruction in a school; other practices will take creative adaptation. Both are workable.

Step 2.1: Set up a Note-Catcher

This step seems rudimentary, but in our experience, it merits stating. Establish a collaborative space where members of the team can catch their notes, ideas, and questions as they explore different K–12 computer science resources online. You might set up a shared spreadsheet, for instance, with a tab for each person on the team, using column headers like resource name, URL, interest level (scale of 1 to 10), ideas for potential use, and other thoughts. Give members of the team a set amount of time to capture their own lists and notes. Then set a window of time for them to review others' as well.

Step 2.2: Scour the Web

Your team's list of potential resources can be populated in lots of ways. First, there are websites devoted to computer science in K–12 spaces like Code.org, CodeAcademy.org, and Mouse.org. Spend time in such spaces checking out examples and experimenting with activities, always asking how what you are seeing might be used to deepen and expand current content-area practice. Second, there are many excellent products on the market that can be used in one's classroom practice. For example, Gerald introduced Tom to mBot robots and that led to the BardBots project where students program robots to perform Shakespeare. Or consider the shelves and shelves of new products that introduce children to coding, robotics, engineering, and more. Explore those products critically and creatively. Again, don't limit your thinking to what the product is intended to do. Focus instead on how it could be creatively used in one's instruction to deepen and expand classroom practice. Third, we suggest checking out videos on YouTube and TED that explore topics of computer science, engineering, and coding. Yes, such videos sometimes come from the perspective of K–12 computer science for its own sake. But if you look past that you might hear or see little insights that can resonate with your students and teachers.

Step 2.3: Reconvene

After a set time has elapsed, everyone should reconvene—ideally around a physical table at the end of which is a big screen and computer with the live document. Prior to the reconvening, members of the team should not only have filled out their findings and notes on their spreadsheet tab. They should also have had a chance to review what their colleagues found, coming to the table with specific ideas about what might be worth exploring further. As everyone shares, keep track of patterns of comments and insights.

Step 2.4: Identify Promising Practices

We emphasize the word *promising*. If your collective goal is to leverage existing curriculum and culture in your classroom, school, and district, then you want to identify the practices (and products associated with them) that you think could meaningfully deepen and expand the current classroom instruction. No solution can be unboxed. Rather, you want to emphasize that there are exciting ideas and products and practices out there already, all of which are waiting for adaptation and application. Ideally, the team leaves the meeting having identified some high-level idea of where computationality might work best to start. For example, a team might say: We want to see how robotics might be used in history class to bring great battles to life for students. Or something like: We want to see if there are creative ways for students to collect more of their own experiential and cultural data for use in science and math classes. Your team might find the following instrument helpful.

Phase 2: Explore | Planning Guide

Date: _____   School/District: _____

What are some of the most interesting resources you reviewed (including your own list)?	
1. Name of resource	2. What made it interesting

Getting Started

3. What are three promising practices you see emerging?	4. What aspects of the respective content area might these practices deepen and expand?
A.	A.
B.	B.
C.	C.

 Awesome! You should now have a more concrete understanding of what kinds of practices might be worth exploring. But before you go piloting anything, take a step back and look at your curriculum as it currently stands. Let's move forward to Phase 3: Connect.

 ## Phase 3: Connect

Nobody wants to waste their time. That goes for students in desks and teachers in their classrooms. So it's important to take a step back and look at what is already required in terms of learning and teaching. Most of us have experienced what happens when this simple step goes unacknowledged. A new initiative or mandate comes raining down from the state or the district or the school and everyone rushes to comply. The result is seldom what anyone would say is best for students' learning. We will say it again and again: Computer science in K–12 spaces cannot be implemented well if it is imposed from without for its own sake. The result will be inherently inequitable, unsustainable, and a pale version of what it could have been if it began instead by honoring current classroom instruction. So, how does one proceed? Well, like this.

Step 3.1: Examine Your Current Curricula

Your current curricula is likely informed by many inputs, including state standards, professional learning organizations' frameworks, and testing data. It might take the form of curriculum maps for grades and content areas, or even key assessments and projects fleshed out in some detail. They might exist in filing cabinets, digital archives, and floppy disks. What's most important in this phase is that the team collectively agrees on how to get it all out on the table—literally, if necessary. For each standard or essential question or goal articulated, ask yourselves: How might computationality deepen and expand this? Remember, for us, what drives the need for computer science in K–12 settings is civically and economically motivated. If it helps, look back at the *why* your team articulated in Phase 1.

Step 3.2: Identify Places in Your Curricula for Embedding Computationality

As you scan through existing curricula, you are looking for places where computationality might be able to deepen and expand instruction. It might be that there are particular priority standards your school is focused on. Or, it could be that there are some current assignment or projects that could use renovation. Whatever the case, it is not a matter of looking for an opening to slip in some computer science. That would be a mistake. Instead, it is about looking honestly at the content-area practices already underway and thinking creatively about how computationality might be leveraged. List those places out for the team to see.

Step 3.3: Ideate Variations of Promising Practices for Piloting

At this point, the team will want to look back at the promising practices from Phase 2 and cross-reference them with the list of potential curricular places you just identified. Discuss explicitly what value computationality might add to the content-area instruction. Engage with the teachers who might be involved with implementation, and gauge their interest—and their hesitations. Ultimately, the team will want to identify at least one or two pilot sites with a clearly articulated goal. For instance: *In February, Mr. Lynch will pilot an assignment while teaching* Romeo and Juliet *in which students write mixed literary analyses. We are interested in better understanding how computational methods of analyzing literature affect students' depth of knowledge about the text and the quality of their written arguments.* With a couple of those pilot ideas in hand, the classroom, school, or district will be well positioned to bring computationality to life in a way that is authentic to its organizational and professional culture.

Phase 3: Connect | Planning Guide

Date: _____   School/District: _____

1. Based on your review of existing documents and priorities, what are some of the potential places where piloting computationality might make sense?

Getting Started

> **2. What are some of the possible promising practices from your exploration of K–12 computer science education that might be worth considering to pilot?**
>
>
>
> *Awesome! Now you have a sense of what some pilots might look like and where they might happen. Let's get into Phase 4: Pilot.*

Phase 4: Pilot

There are many ways to pilot instructional innovations in classrooms, schools, and districts. One of the most thorough ways to do so is through a methodology referred to broadly as action research. Action research refers to the systematic investigation of how changes in practice affect one's teaching and learning. Resources to support action research in the classroom abound and are just an online search away. If the idea of a robust model is intimidating, we might suggest instead a simple approach to get started.

Step 4.1: Identify and Align Resources

Once the team has identified places to pilot computational methods in specific classrooms, it's vital to step back and ask: What resources will we need to make this happen well? Resources can refer to many things. First, consider time. What kind of time is necessary for the people involved to pilot this? There is the instructional time already blocked during class periods. But there might also need to be time to plan, especially with other colleagues who might support the efforts. For instance, if a teacher was going to try to use robots to teach Shakespeare, she might want to huddle up with the school's technology support lead to review the ins and outs of implementing robots in the classroom. In the example of Shakespearean robots, it's also necessary to plan for the peripheral materials needed, like laptops. Second, consider money. What kind of funding is necessary for the people involved to pull this off? Funding relates to two main resources: people and products. If additional planning and meeting will be needed to implement the pilot project, then consider whether compensation would be fair and available. But the people are only part of it. If specific products are needed, then that, too, might require lining up in advance. Products like necessary technologies will be clear, but other related costs might not be. We suggest mapping low-, medium-, and high-level potential costs.

Step 4.2: Observe Classroom Practice

Members of the team should schedule times to visit colleagues who are implementing pilots. The purpose of the visits is not to evaluate. Rather, the purpose is to offer collegial feedback about the work, which might take the form of questions or other kinds of insights. By making the time to observe, the team can help those teachers piloting computationality feel supported. Schools and districts often have protocols for conducting observations, many of which can be adapted for these visits. Just remember that this isn't a formal observation or anything like that. It's a collegial observation with the goal of helping the teacher and team better understand some of the nuances of what embedding computer science takes in your setting.

Step 4.3: Check in Periodically with the Team

Whether it is through email updates or face-to-face meetings, it's important to update the team on how the pilot is going. Such updates can be solicited from the team lead or can be shared by the teacher directly. The purpose of the updates is to keep the work energized and on everyone's radars. It is easy in the daily dynamics of working in schools to lose sight of something like a pilot. When stacked against other demands for time and mental energy, something like a pilot (especially one focused on K–12 computer science) might be hard-pressed to make the cut in the moment. By scheduling solicited or proactive updates, you can better ensure that the community remains primed to learn and grow together.

Phase 4: Pilot | Planning Guide

Date: _____   School/District: _____

1. What resources will you need to get this pilot off the ground? Think about not just money but also materials and time and people.

Getting Started

> **2. When are members of the team going to visit the pilot teacher in action? Take a moment now to write down specific dates, times, and locations.**
>
>
>
> **3. When and how is the team going to check in collectively during the pilot? Who is going to make sure you do it? Hash it out here.**
>
>
>
> *Sweet! Now you have a thoughtful pilot underway. Great job. When you're ready, let's go to Phase 5: Evaluate.*

 ## Phase 5: Evaluate

So, how did the pilot go? What lessons can the team learn about how to use computer science to deepen and expand content-area instruction? Those are the key questions to consider in this phase. It is not uncommon for teachers to try out new things. Good teachers do that all the time. But it is less than common in many schools for a team to sit around the table, look at student work, hear from the teacher's perspective, and then extract from those data some principles of practice that can be used to frame work going forward. But that's the goal here.

Step 5.1: Begin with Student Artifacts

Few activities have the power to ground our conversations about learning and teaching like looking at student work. As the team convenes, the pilot teacher should bring some artifacts of student work that emerged from the previous few weeks. Then, use a protocol for looking at student work for the team to examine the artifact. What questions and insights does it surface? After the team gets a chance to unpack the artifact, the pilot teacher can fill in gaps and answer questions. Be sure to avoid high-inference observations. Keep it low-inference: concrete, rooted only in the artifact.

Step 5.2: Capture Teachers' Feedback

After focusing on the assignment, open the discussion up more broadly to solicit feedback from the pilot teacher. Use whatever protocol your school or district already has. The kinds of questions can vary, of course. But here are a few to get you started: What are the big lessons learned about the possibilities for computationality in the classroom, school, and district? What would have made the project even more successful? What key alterations to the assignment might you make knowing what you know now?

Step 5.3: Discuss How to Proceed

This can be a very challenging step for any classroom, school, or district. Very often there can be far too many or far too few clear ways to proceed. You want the former. We suggest creating an opportunity for the team to think broadly and creatively. Get all ideas for procession on the table, or better yet on a white board with lots of colors and shapes and arrows. Don't dismiss any idea. Then step back and look at all the possibilities.

Phase 5: Evaluate | Planning Guide

Date: _____   School/District: _____

1. What student work do you have before you, and what does it tell you about the depth of students' learning? What questions does the work raise for you about the potential for computationality to deepen and expand the content area?

Getting Started

> **2. What does the lead teacher have to say about the ups and downs of the pilot? What potential does the teacher see? What lessons did the teacher learn?**
>
>
>
> **3. After brainstorming any and all possible ways to proceed, what is sticking and why? Capture it here.**
>
>
>
> ✋ *Yes! Now it's time to strategize how you are going to expand and sustain this work. That's what Phase 6: Expand is all about.*

Phase 6: Expand

Based on team's evaluation of the pilot, you should now have some rich insights into what worked, what didn't, and what possibilities lie before you as a professional community. The final phase is to begin expanding those insights. We have identified three main steps to take.

Step 6.1: Identify a Strategy for Expanding Horizontally and/or Vertically

Schools and districts tend to have similar organizational structures. When it comes to expanding computationality in yours, leverage those structures. The main ways to think about expansion tend to be horizontally (spreading the work across grades) or vertically (spreading the work throughout departments). Which works best has a lot to do with the people and practices already underway in your setting. If there are individual teachers in other grades who seem keen to explore computationality, then proceeding vertically might make sense. Or if teachers in the same department as the pilot teacher are eager to implement their own projects, then that energy is priceless. Both can be effective. Some have suggested that departmentally similar teachers might be worth targeting for expansion, especially if they teach different grade levels than the pilot teachers. We'll leave that up to you.

Step 6.2: Orient New Collaborators with the Process to Date

Whoever you invite to expand the use of computational methods in your setting, be sure to create a space for them to become oriented with the team's work to date. Of particular importance is drawing their attention to that critical and reflective work from Phase 1 where the team ruptured their assumptions about why computer science might be worth pursuing in the first place. There are myriad ways to do this. What is most important is to avoid the pitfall of essentially telling someone they are expected to integrate computational methods into their practice without rooting that work to a higher sense of purpose that deepens and expands content-area practice.

Step 6.3: Establish a Computationality Committee to Maintain the Work

In order to systematize the expansion and sustainability of computational methods in your setting, it is at this point that we recommend establishing a computationality committee. The idea is for key leads from the initial pilot team to establish a regular meeting schedule in which they gather to review artifacts of students' and teachers' work, reveal problems and possibilities, and establish next steps. In addition to these formal foci, the committee can work informally to share examples of what computationality looks like in classrooms with other teachers, parents, and students. The idea is to slowly and steadily socialize the idea that computationality is a rich addition to any content area and grade level.

Phase 6: Expand | Planning Guide

Date: _____ School/District: _____

1. How is your setting organized, and what makes the most sense in terms of expanding the work? Vertical or horizontal or both?

Getting Started

2. What do new committee members and participants need to know about the conversations the team has had already? Share notes and anything else that will give them context.

3. Who should serve on the computationality committee? How often will they meet, and what are their core goals for the next three, six, and nine months?

 You've done it. You have started to get started. Beautiful job.

Conclusions and Beginnings

In this chapter, we have offered a brief and broad series of suggestions for getting started with computationality in your classroom, school, or district. Our hunch is that you will have your own ways to go about this based on your existing organizational and cultural structures. Still, by reading through our lowest-common-denominator suggestions, we hope that we might have revealed some angles or questions that you and your team might not have yet considered.

We would be remiss to leave you here without mentioning that there are professional corners where others think and talk about this work. We have alluded to several throughout the book, but allow us to draw your attention to two. First, the International Society for Technology in Education (ISTE) does an excellent job in bringing together teachers and leaders who are thinking passionately about the role of technology in education. Their online community and professional learning resources are well worth engaging. Second, CSforALL is emerging as a powerful and useful unifying organization in K–12 computer science education. They are, as we are, committed to the idea that computationality is vital for civic and economic engagement. Their online resources and live conferences are wonderful supports to teachers and school and district leaders. Look up both organizations on Google to learn more.

From politics to chessboards, from Houston to New York, we have tried to make the case that computer science is a vital area for focused exploration—so vital that we have to stop calling it computer science. We have argued that it is better to think in terms of computationality as computational methods and logic mediate more and more of our world. Young people and their teachers need ubiquitous, critical, and creative exposure to computationality. We believe wholly that computationality can deepen and expand one's classroom practice in any grade and any discipline. Our belief, however, is not driven by technophilia. Quite the opposite.

In her poem *Boy Breaking Glass*, poet Gwendolyn Brooks writes, "I shall create! If not a note, a hole. // If not an overture, a desecration." To paraphrase the poem's speaker, our belief is driven by undying faith in the power of human beings to create both notes and holes, overtures and desecrations. Like the speaker in the poem, we think human beings are inherently creative—but that creativity can be put to positive and negative ends. Computationality is itself a product of human creativity, but whether it will create notes and overtures remains to be seen. We have our doubts at times. But we also have hope. We are hopeful that the more teachers, leaders, and students come to understand computationality as a way of engaging with the world—not just scientific and mathematical corners of the academy—the more likely we are to witness a sea change, one in which computationality serves our highest aspirations for society. Whether or not this book contributes to that change rests entirely in your hands.

Quite literally.

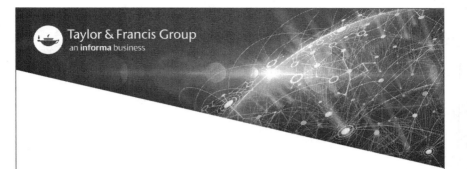